Hello and welcome!
Ich bin der Wordmaster und helfe dir beim Wörterlernen.

Nachdem du neue Wörter in der Schule besprochen hast, kannst du die **New words** *in diesem Buch als Vokabelheft benutzen.*

Die **fett gedruckten** *deutschen Wörter sind Lernwörter. Sie fehlen im englischen Satz, damit du sie eintragen kannst.*

Meine Tipps

1 *Die Reihenfolge der* **New words** *entspricht der Reihenfolge der neuen Wörter im Vocabulary deines Schülerbuches. Dort kannst du deine Lösungen überprüfen.*

2 *Wenn du mal nicht weiter weißt, kannst du auch im Vocabulary nachschauen.*

3 *Lern neue Wörter in einem Satz. So kann man sie sich besser merken.*

4 *Üb den neuen Wortschatz. Deck zum Beispiel mit einem Blatt Papier die englischen Sätze ab und versuch, die deutschen Sätze ins Englische zu übersetzen. Oder umgekehrt.*

New words ▸ p. 1

Mein **Name** ist ...

Ich komme aus Deutschland.

Ich gehe zur **Schule.**

Ich **lerne** Englisch.

Unser **Lehrer** ist nett.

My *name* is ...

I'm from Germany.

I go to *school* .

I _____ English.

Our _____ is nice.

Hi! *Ich bin Ken und gebe dir Tipps. Zum Beispiel ...*

Überhaupt: Es gibt neben **New words** *viele lustige Übungen. Die Lösungen findest du im beigelegten Heftchen.*

... das große R bedeutet Revision: Auf Deutsch Wiederholung. Hier übst du Vokabeln, die du bereits früher gelernt hast.

Welcome back

1 Numbers and letters: the weather

Zu jeder Zahl gehört ein Buchstabe. Finde die Lösungswörter und dann den „geheimen Satz".

Dear Sophie,

Scotland is a great country, but the __ __ __ T__ __ __ __ (5 11 15 8 1 11 13) here is really awful. It's the middle of

August and it's __ __ __ __ (3 6 14 9) and __ __ __ __ __ (13 15 12 2 4) every day. We never see the S__ __ (7 10 2) because

there are so many big, black __ __ __ __ __ __ (3 14 6 10 9 7). We were in the __ __ __ __ __ __ __ __ (16 6 10 2 8 15 12 2 7)

last week and there was __ __ __ __ (7 2 6 5) there! That's mad – __ __ __ __ (7 2 6 5) in summer. At least there

were no __ __ __ __ __ __ (7 8 6 13 16 7). I'm sure your holiday was much better. Majorca is usually a

G__ __ __ __ P__ __ __ __ __ (17 6 6 9 | 18 14 15 3 11) for W__ __ __ __ (5 15 13 16) and __ __ __ __ __ (7 10 2 2 4) __ __ __ __ __ __ __ (5 11 15 8 1 11 13).

Say hi to the others. See you soon.

Tim

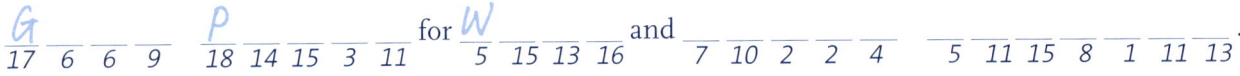

The secret sentence:

__ __ __ __ (5 12 2 9) __ __ __ __ (15 2 9) __ __ __ __ (13 15 12 2), __ __ __ __ __ __ (3 14 6 10 9 7)

__ __ __ (15 2 9) __ __ __ __ (7 2 6 5) __ __ __ __ __ (1 10 13 13 4) __ __ (10 18)!

__ __ __ (12 8 7), __ __ __ __ __ __ (8 12 16 11 8 6) __ __ __ (17 6)!

2 The fourth word

Welches Wort fehlt hier?

1	loud – quiet	hot – *cold*	6	storm – stormy	cloud – _____
2	empty – full	cool – _____	7	met – meet	threw – _____
3	windy – wind	rainy – _____	8	sport – do	photos – _____
4	this – these	that – _____	9	drink – drank	ride – _____
5	July – summer	January – _____	10	Bristol – city	Germany – _____

New words ▸ pp. 6 – 7

Letztes Jahr **reisten** wir nach Cornwall. — Last year we _____ to Cornwall.

Unsere Freunde hatten dort einen **Wohnwagen**. — Our friends had a _____ there.

Aber wir hatten ein Haus **am** Meer. — But we had a house _____ sea.

Wir waren jeden Tag **am Strand**. — We were _____ every day.

Wir **blieben** dort stundenlang. — We _____ there for hours.

Es war oft kalt, aber wir blieben **trotzdem**. — It was often cold, but we stayed _____ .

In der Stadt gab es ein kleines **Theater**. — There was a small _____ in the town.

Heute ist es sehr **kühl** draußen. — It's very _____ outside today.

Lass uns morgen **einen Spaziergang machen**. — Let's _____ tomorrow.

Aus welchem **Land** kommst du? — What _____ do you come from?

Fliegst du oft nach London? — Do you often _____ to London?

Von hier haben wir eine großartige **Aussicht**. — We've got a great _____ from here.

Kann ich mein Handy **im Flugzeug** benutzen? — Can I use my mobile _____ ?

Sophie schaute im ganzen Zimmer **umher**. — Sophie looked all _____ the room.

Es ist heiß hier, wenn die Sonne **scheint**. — It's hot here when the sun __ _____ .

Mallorca ist eine schöne **Insel**. — Majorca is a beautiful _____ .

Der **Himmel** war gestern so blau. — The _____ was so blue yesterday.

Wir haben unseren **eigenen** Strand. — We've got our _____ beach.

Meistens **fahren** wir **mit dem Rad** dorthin. — We usually _____ there _____ .

Lasst uns **etwas** Neues unternehmen. — Let's do _____ new.

Diese Farben **passen** nicht **zusammen**. — These colours don't _____ .

Wie war das Wetter? — _____ ?

3 Odd word out

Ein Wort passt nicht. Finde und unterstreiche es.

1 sunny – cloudy – <u>sun</u> – stormy

2 library – village – city – town

3 shirt – glasses – dress – shorts

4 hall – kitchen – bedroom – stage

5 bridge – caravan – tower – church

6 she – into – from – under

4 Lost words

Ergänze die Sätze mit den Wörtern aus den Luftballons.

1 It's warm outside. Let's go ___for___ a walk.

2 Look! There are lots of people _____ the beach.

3 Are you scared _____ cold water?

4 The Shaws travelled _____ Cornwall on Saturday.

5 They're staying _____ a caravan.

6 We've got a nice holiday flat _____ the sea.

7 Jack is staying _____ home this summer.

8 We can go _____ town and watch some street theatre.

5 Word snake

Zwölf deutsche Wörter sind in der Schlange versteckt.
Schreibe die englischen Übersetzungen auf.

1 _____ 4 _____ 7 _____ 10 _____

2 _____ 5 _____ 8 _____ 11 _____

3 _____ 6 _____ 9 _____ 12 _____

6 Word pairs

Welche Wörter passen zusammen?

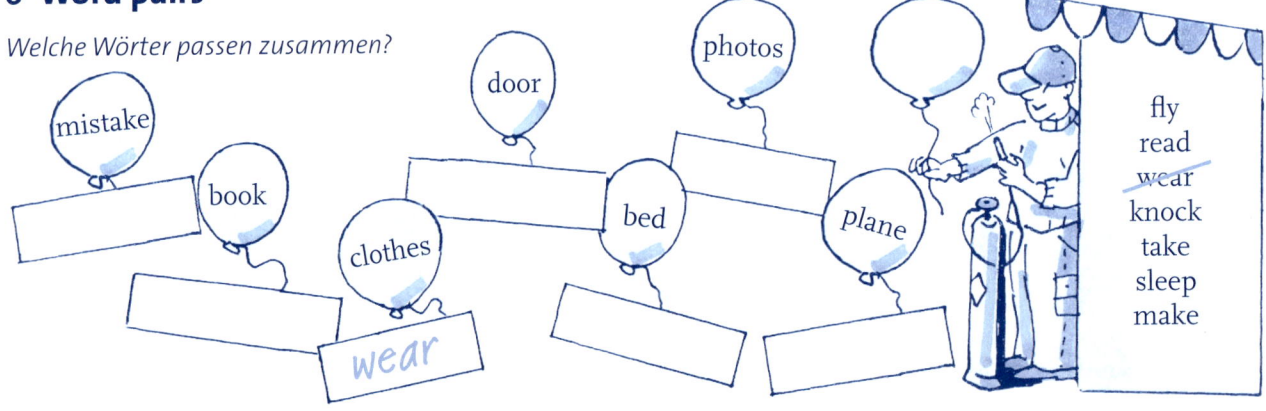

7 Spot the mistakes

In jedem Satz gibt es zwei Fehler. Unterstreiche und korrigiere sie.

1 Dan eated too much at Anandas birthday party. ⎯⎯ *ate* ⎯⎯ ⎯⎯ *Ananda's* ⎯⎯

2 We flied to Paris last yier.

3 Yesterday we rided to school by baik.

4 I saw she when I comed into the room.

5 She taked the pencil and put it into her pencil cais.

6 I meeted two childs in the park yesterday.

8 Bits and pieces

Setze die Bruchstücke zusammen, um Wörter zu bilden, denen Du in dieser Unit begegnet bist. Übersetze sie ins Deutsche.

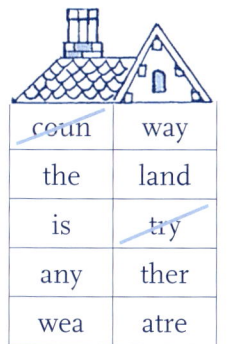

coun	way
the	land
is	try
any	ther
wea	atre

1 *country – Land*

2 _____

3 _____

4 _____

5 _____

post	van
cara	tain
tra	thing
some	card
moun	vel

6 _____

7 _____

8 _____

9 _____

10 _____

9 What's the word: *much* or *many*?

a) Durchstreiche das falsche Wort:
much *oder* many.

1 How much / many days can you stay?

2 I haven't got much / many time.

3 There isn't much / many chicken in
the fridge.

4 Are there much / many sausages?

5 Use *much/many*
with plural words!

b) Vervollständige die Sätze mit den richtigen Wörtern.

1 You can hear so much new _____ on the radio.
(songs / music)

2 We have to do too many _____ for school.
(exercises / homework)

3 I don't know very much _____ .
(English grammar / English words)

4 How much _____ have we got in the cupboard?
(biscuits / bread)

5 I haven't got many _____ .
(free time / hobbies)

New words ▸ pp. 8–9

Heute ist es nicht warm – nur 12 **Grad**.

It isn't warm today – only 12 _____ .

Es ist regnerisch aber nicht **neblig**.

It's rainy, but not _____ .

Nebel mag ich wirklich nicht.

I really don't like _____ .

Warum bist du so **traurig**?

Why are you so _____ ?

Keiner hat Zeit für mich.

_____ has got time for me.

Dan **spricht** jeden Tag **mit** Jo.

Dan _____ Jo every day.

Brauchst du neue **Kleider**?

Do you need new _____ ?

Lasst uns im **See** schwimmen.

Let's swim in the _____ .

Kann ich dich morgen **besuchen**?

Can I _____ you tomorrow?

10 Crossword: words and pictures

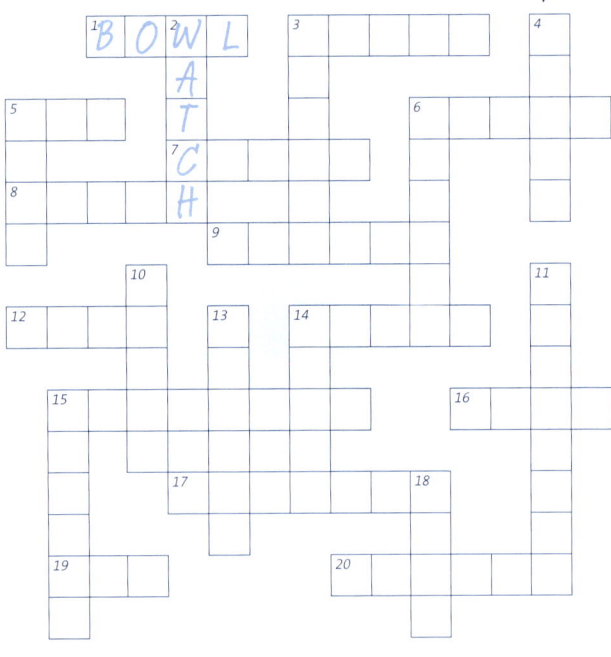

Across

1 Can I have a ★ for my fruit salad? (4)
3 There are three sandwiches on the ★. (5)
5 another word for 'child'(3)
6 the English word for 'Brot' (5)
7 Please get up! It's seven o' ★. (5)
8 the singular of teeth (5)
9 land with water round it (6)
12 Listen! That's the door ★. There's somebody at the front door. (4)
14 You can visit the Eiffel ★ in Paris. (5)
15 The highest ★ is Mount Everest. (8)
16 the English word for 'Socke'(4)
17 You need them to see better. (7)
19 hand – arm / foot – ★ (3)
20 Can you play the ★? (6)

Down

2

3

4

5

6

10

11

13

14

15

18

11 Word search

Finde die englischen Wörter im Gitter und vervollständige sie in den Boxen.
Dann übersetze sie. Alle Wörter hast du in der 5. Klasse gelernt. (   )

Clothes

top   Oberteil
_ o _ _ _
s _ _ _ _
_ h o _ _ _ _
s _ c _ _ _ _
_ r _ _ _

Family

_ _ n _ _
_ d _ _ _ _ _
_ r _ _
_ _ _ n _ _
_ d _ _
_ _ c _ _ _

School

_ e _ _ _ _ _ _
_ _ u _ _ _ _ _
b o _ _ _
_ _ _ _ e _ _ _ _ _
_ _ _ k _ _
_ l _ _ _ _ _

Parts of the body

_ _ _ _ d _
t _ _ _ _ _ _
_ e _ _ _
_ _ g _
_ o _ _
_ o _ _

C	R	I	S	P	S	C	W	Q	B	I	S	C	U	I	T
H	D	T	O	O	T	H	S	A	U	S	A	G	E	Q	T
I	S	Q	P	T	O	E	F	S	O	V	G	G	R	W	I
C	Y	B	G	Q	H	E	Y	H	Q	I	S	R	M	B	M
K	S	A	U	N	T	S	A	I	U	P	T	A	I	O	E
E	O	F	I	S	H	E	D	R	J	A	U	N	C	O	T
N	C	G	X	J	P	B	A	T	C	R	D	D	E	T	A
V	K	R	M	L	O	O	U	F	L	R	E	P	M	S	B
J	S	A	O	E	T	A	G	H	A	O	N	A	B	R	L
U	D	N	U	G	A	R	H	A	S	T	T	R	X	A	E
N	R	D	T	M	T	D	T	N	S	D	U	E	S	B	W
C	B	C	H	N	O	M	E	D	R	R	A	N	H	B	M
L	R	H	E	M	Q	J	R	V	T	O	P	T	O	I	O
E	E	I	A	C	H	I	L	D	R	E	N	S	E	T	U
C	A	L	D	T	E	A	C	H	E	R	Q	F	S	T	S
H	K	D	H	D	R	E	S	S	S	N	A	K	E	E	E

Pets

_ n _ _ _ _
_ _ _ _ t _
r _ _ _ _
m _ u _ _
_ i _ _
_ h

Food

_ _ e _ _ _
_ h _ _ _ _ _
b _ _ _ _ _ _ _
_ _ p _ _
_ o _ _
_ s _

Unit 1

New words ▸ *p. 11*

Lass uns heute in der **Kantine** essen.	Let's eat in the _____ today.
Bitte **beschreibe** das Bild.	Please _____ the picture.
Das ist eine gute **Beschreibung**.	That's a good _____ .
Du kannst Berge im **Hintergrund** sehen.	You can see mountains in the _____ .
Und die Zwillinge sind im **Vordergrund**.	And the twins are in the _____ .
Ich mag das Foto **unten** auf der Seite.	I like the photo _____ of the page.

1 Word families

Finde die passenden Nomen zu den angegebenen Verben.

1 rehearse *rehearsal*

2 describe _____

3 drink _____

4 invite _____

5 live _____

6 dance _____

2 · What are the words?

Wo ist Ken?

a) near the lake
b) next to the lake

a) in the middle
b) on the left

a) in front of the tree
b) behind the tree

a) at the top of the mountain
b) at the bottom of the mountain

a) in the foreground
b) in the background

a) under water
b) between the two children

New words ▸ p. 12

Wieviel kostet dein **Flug** nach New York?

How much is your _____ to New York?

Darf ich das nächste **Mal** mitkommen?

May I come with you next _____ ?

Unser Urlaub war **etwas** zu kurz.

Our holiday was _____ too short.

Lass uns mit der **U-Bahn** fahren.

Let's go by _____ .

So viele Autos! Diese Straße ist **gefährlich**.

So many cars! This road is _____ .

Diese Autos sind zu **schnell**.

These cars are too _____ .

Die Züge in England sind manchal **langsam**.

Trains in England are sometimes _____ .

Was ist **das Beste** am Film?

What's _____ about the film?

Ich mochte die **Gebäude** in New York.

I liked the _____ in New York.

Wir sind mit dem **Fahrstuhl** nach oben gefahren.

We took the _____ to the top.

Wir hatten eine **unglaubliche** Aussicht.

We had an _____ view.

Von oben kann man **meilenweit** sehen.

You can see _____ from the top.

Wie viele Meter hat eine **Meile**?

How many metres are there in a _____ ?

3 Crossword

Trage in das Rätsel die simple past-Formen der angegebenen Verben ein.

Haufig brauchst du nur *-ed* anzuhängen, um die simple past zu bilden.

Aber Vorsicht! Die unregelmäßigen Vergangheitsformen solltest du extra lernen.

Hier kannst du das schon mal üben ...

Across

1 get	*14* hurt
4 ride	*16* drink
6 go	*18* do
8 eat	*19* throw
10 meet	
12 sit	
13 have	

Down

1 give	*10* make
2 take	*11* tell
3 see	*12* swim
4 run	*14* hear
5 come	*15* read
7 teach	*17* know
9 put	

New words ▸ *p. 13*

Das geht dich gar nichts an.

_____ .

Na los, komm! Wir haben nicht viel Zeit.

_____ ! We haven't got much time.

Ich will nicht **unhöflich** sein.

I don't want to be _____ .

4 Scrambled words

Finde in den Buchstabenrätseln die fehlenden Gebäude oder Bauwerke und vervollständige die Sätze.

1 On Sundays some people go to ★. ___ ___ ___ ___ ___ ___

2 There's a new play at the ★. ___ ___ ___ ___ ___ ___ ___

3 Does that ★ sell fruit? ___ ___ ___ ___

4 Dan and his friends go to Cotham ★. ___ ___ ___ ___ ___ ___

5 Yesterday we climbed Cabot ★. ___ ___ ___ ___ ___

6 The boat trip ends at the next ★. ___ ___ ___ ___ ___ ___

7 Do I get off the train at this ★? ___ ___ ___ ___ ___ ___ ___

8 There are lots of books in this ★. ___ ___ ___ ___ ___ ___ ___

9 How much are the tickets for the ★? ___ ___ ___ ___ ___ ___

10 Sophie lives in a big ★ in Bristol. ___ ___ ___ ___ ___

CCHHRU

TAHERET

HOPS

CHLOOS

TEORW

BDEGIR

SINOATT

LABIRRY

MEUMSU

EHOSU

The secret word is ___ ___ ___ ___ ___ ___ ___ ___

5 The fourth word

Welches Wort fehlt hier?

1 left – right / background – _____

2 full – empty / fast – _____

3 up – down / at the top – _____

4 forget – forgot / know – _____

5 before – after / in front of – _____

6 hand – finger / foot – _____

7 they – their / she – _____

8 bird – cage / rabbit – _____

9 invite – invitation / describe – _____

10 give – gave / teach – _____

6 Odd word out

Ein Wort passt nicht. Finde und unterstreiche es

1 good – fantastic – <u>dangerous</u> – great

2 table – bedroom – wardrobe – desk

3 chicken – cheese – bread – cooker

4 cat – children – mice – women

5 loud – climb – follow – help

6 theatre – church – bike – library

7 badminton – table tennis – cards – basketball

8 knew – go – taught – met

7 Word search

Finde 20 Adjektive im Gitter und bilde 10 Gegensatzpaare. (   )

E	A	S	Y	N	I	C	E	V	J	R	I
S	W	A	R	M	D	B	A	D	N	O	N
G	B	O	R	I	N	G	G	R	E	A	T
O	N	N	R	O	V	E	S	U	R	D	E
O	F	C	O	L	D	C	Z	E	U	I	R
D	T	O	W	O	N	O	N	D	D	F	E
N	Q	U	I	E	T	O	Z	C	E	F	S
T	E	R	R	I	B	L	E	F	V	I	T
G	W	R	O	N	G	L	N	A	O	C	I
N	R	I	G	H	T	H	M	S	G	U	N
S	L	O	W	L	W	O	K	T	N	L	G
L	O	U	D	Y	K	T	R	D	H	T	O

1 *interesting*   *boring*

2 _ _ _ _ _ t   _ _ r _ _ _ _

3 _ o _ _   _ _ d

4 _ _ _ _ y   d _ _ _ _ _ _ _ _

5 g _ _ _ _ _   _ _ u _

6 _ _ t   c _ _ _ _

7 _ _ c _   _ _ d _

8 _ _ g _ _ _   _ r _

9 _ _ o _   w _ _ _

10 _ _ _ _ t   _ _ _ w

8 Word snail

Übersetze die Wörter ins Englische. Trage die englischen Wörter in die Wortschnecke ein. Die Anfangsbuchstaben in der Schnecke helfen dir.

beschreiben   gefährlich   Hintergrund   See   zwischen   langsam   sprechen   Kleider   Herd   neblig   Flug   unhöflich

The secret words are: ▢▢▢▢▢ ▢▢ ▢▢▢▢▢▢▢

New words *▶ pp. 14 – 20*

Glaubst du das wirklich?	_____
Ich will im Bett bleiben. – **Kommt nicht in Frage!**	I want to stay in bed. – _____
Ach komm – ich bin heute so müde.	_____ – I'm so tired today.
Jack, bitte **beruhige dich**!	Jack, please _____
Warum **wirst** du immer so **wütend**?	Why do you always _____ so _____ ?
Warum ist er so **böse auf** uns?	Why is he so _____ us?
Es gibt **nichts** mehr zu sagen.	There's _____ more to say.
Warum magst du keine **Rollenspiele**?	Why don't you like _____ ?
Welche **Bindewörter** kennt ihr?	Which _____ do you know?
Ist **Frau** Smith verheiratet?	Is _____ Smith married?
Wie lang ist die Mittagspause? – Eine **Stunde**.	How long is the lunch break? One _____ .
Unser Lehrer ist eine sehr freundliche **Person**.	Our teacher is a very friendly _____ .
Warum **ist** das Licht **an**? Es ist nicht sehr dunkel.	Why _____ the light _____ ? It isn't very dark.
Frage jemanden, **der** Englisch spricht.	_____ speaks English.

9 Plurals

Vervollständige die Tabelle.

Krokodil, crocodile, crocodiles

	German	Singular	Plural
1	Mann	man	men
2		woman	
3	Zahn		
4		child	
5		photo	
6	Kartoffel		
7		quiz	
8	Kasten		

	German	Singular	Plural
9		life	
10		hero	
11			mice
12	Fuß		
13		country	
14	Aufsatz		
15			families
16	Hobby		

10 Picture puzzle

Finde 7 weitere Dinge.

elephant

_____

_____

_____   _____

_____   _____

_____

11 Word ladder

Bewege dich von Sprosse zu Sprosse, um nach oben zu kommen.
Bei jeder Sprosse darfst du nur einen Buchstaben ändern.

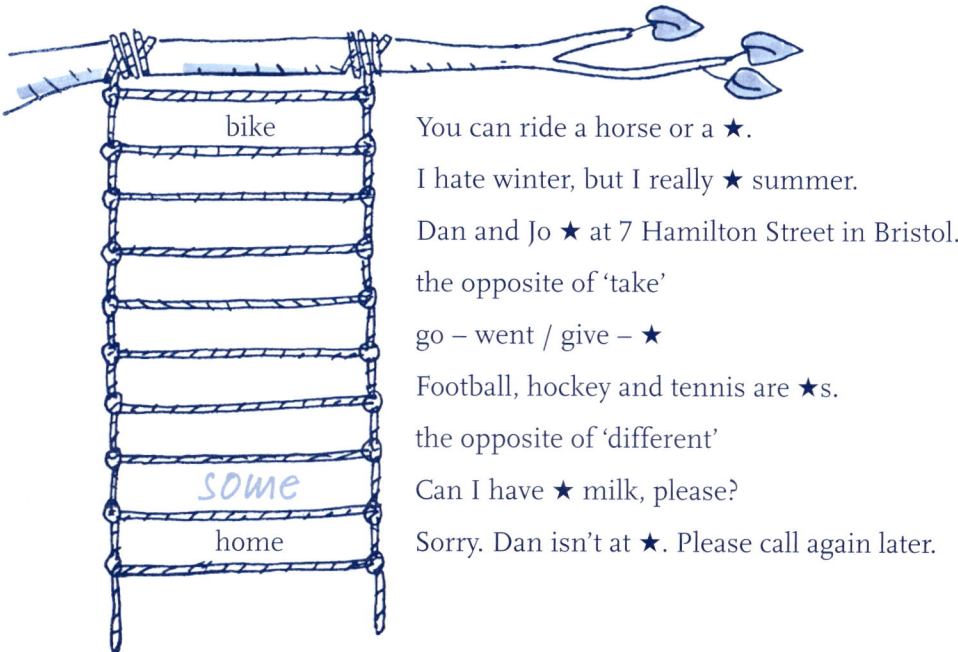

bike

You can ride a horse or a ★.

I hate winter, but I really ★ summer.

Dan and Jo ★ at 7 Hamilton Street in Bristol.

the opposite of 'take'

go – went / give – ★

Football, hockey and tennis are ★s.

the opposite of 'different'

some — Can I have ★ milk, please?

home — Sorry. Dan isn't at ★. Please call again later.

12 Lost words

Vervollständige die Sätze mit jeweils einem Wort aus dem rechten oder linken Hantelgewicht.

1 I can't sleep when the **light** is **on**.

2 Do you like the photo at the _____ _____ the page?

3 Please _____ _____ . There's no reason to shout.

4 I think the best _____ _____ school is PE and games.

5 Would you like to go _____ a _____ in the park?

6 There's a great view from here. You can see _____ _____ .

7 If you don't want to walk, we can go _____ _____ .

8 Mum is _____ _____ me because I dropped an expensive plate.

about	bottom
by	calm
down	car
for	light
for	miles
with	thing
of	angry
on	walk

New words ▸ *pp. 22 – 23*

Sie **rettete** das Leben des kleinen Mädchens.
She _____ the little girl's life.

Der Räuber kam **durch** das Fenster hinein.
The robber came in _____ the window.

Ein **Etagenbett!** Ich will oben schlafen.
A _____ ! I want to sleep at the top.

Ich sah ihn nicht, aber ich **konnte** ihn hören.
I didn't see him, but I _____ hear him.

Kannst du bitte mein Handy **holen**?
Can you _____ my mobile please?

Ich muss mich verabschieden, **bevor** ich gehe.
I have to say goodbye _____ I go.

Nachdem ich rufe, kannst du kommen.
_____ I call you can come.

Wie **weit** ist es zum Strand? – Zwei Meilen.
How _____ is it to the beach? – Two miles.

Schau, sie **winkt** uns zu.
Look she'_____ at us.

Räum dein Zimmer auf, oder **du kriegst Ärger.**
Tidy your room or _____ .

Es sind nur **ein paar** Leute am Strand.
There are only _____ people on the beach.

Ist alles **in Ordnung?**
Is everything _____ ?

Besuch uns bald mal wieder!
Come and _____ us again soon!

Ich **weiß** nichts **über** indische Musik.
I _____ nothing _____ Indian music.

Ich mag Geschichten mit einem **Happyend.**
I like stories with a _____ .

Jo kam **rechtzeitig**, aber Dan war zu spät.
Jo came _____ but Dan was late.

Wir können heute nicht **surfen gehen.**
We can't _____ today.

13 Spot the mistakes

In jedem Satz sind zwei Fehler. Unterstreiche und korrigiere sie.

1 What time is your flait too New York?   *flight* _____ _____

2 My father usually gos to work bai bus.   _____ _____

3 Can you sea the children on the park?   _____ _____

4 I haven't got match money, only a few paunds.   _____ _____

5 I'm not really happi about your idee.   _____ _____

6 Finnish your homework bevor you go out.   _____ _____

7 Is your teacher engry when you make misteaks?   _____ _____

14 Word groups

*Trage die Wörter aus der Wiese
in die richtige Blume ein.*

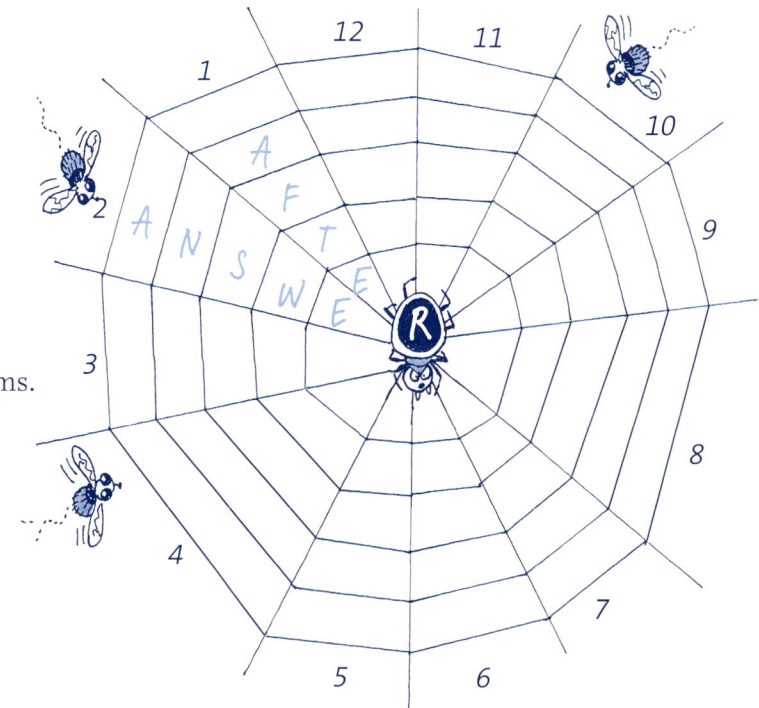

theatre — play

ticket

sports
and
hobbies — skate

head

travel — boat

ship

act bike boat bus car collect stamps ears eyes face go surfing
go swimming hair make models mouth nose plane play
play the guitar rehearse skate scene ship show teeth ticket train

15 Word web

*Vervollständige das Spinnennetz.
Alle Lösungswörter haben 4 bis 6 Buchstaben
und enden auf -R.*

1 the opposite of 'before'
2 the opposite of 'question'
3 You can drink ★ or you can wash with it.
4 Blue is my favourite ★.
5 I don't play the piano, but I play the ★.
6 German students don't usually ★ uniforms.
7 You use a ★ to make a hot lunch.
8 the opposite of 'always'
9 Are your mother and ★ divorced?
10 There are 60 minutes in an ★ .
11 'A' is the first ★ in the alphabet.
12 '27' is a ★.

AFTER
ANSWER
R

Unit 2

New words ▸ *pp. 26 – 27*

Bekommst du genug **Taschengeld**?	Do you get enough _____ ?
Nimm deine Hände aus deinen **Taschen**!	Take your hands out of your _____ !
Jo **gibt** Geld **aus**. Dan **spart** es.	Jo _____ money. Dan _____ it.
Kennst du die Ergebnisse der **Umfrage**?	Do you know the results of the _____ ?
Die **Mütze** und die **Jacke** gefallen mir.	I like the _____ and the _____ .
Warum trägst du nie **Make-up**?	Why do you never wear _____ ?
Ist dein **Pullover** neu?	Is your _____ new?
Nein, aber mein **Rock** ist neu.	No, but my _____ is new?
Ich muss **ein Paar Sportschuhe** kaufen.	I have to buy _____ .
Deine **Hose** ist etwas zu kurz.	Your _____ are a bit too short.

1 Scrambled words: clothes

*Löse die Buchstabenrätsel, um Kleidungsstücke zu finden.
Trage die deutschen Übersetzungen ein. Die markierten
Buchstaben ergeben das „geheime Wort".*

triks	S _ _ _ _	Rock	S
swateihrst	_ _ _ _ _ _ _ _		
tersours	_ _ _ _ _ _ _		
pelloruv	_ _ _ _ _ _ _		
jetcak	_ _ _ _ _		
tarreins	_ _ _ _ _ _ _		

2 Odd word out

Ein Wort passt nicht. Finde und unterstreiche es.

1 thought – found – <u>wear</u> – knew

2 tower – bridge – theatre – beach

3 ship – storm – fog – rain

4 make-up – trousers – jacket – trainers

5 rabbit – budgie – guinea pig – mouse

6 some – a lot – sad – a few

3 Word search

Im Rätsel sind 16 Dinge versteckt, die du in einem Haus finden kannst. (   )

bathroom _____   _____

_____   _____

_____   _____

_____   _____

_____   _____

_____   _____

D	C	S	P	T	C	H	A	I	R	B
O	D	H	R	F	S	T	A	I	R	S	E
O	I	O	B	K	I	T	C	H	E	N	D
R	S	W	A	R	D	R	O	B	E	J	W
O	H	E	Q				C	J	U	I
C	W	R	E				U	P	M	N
O	A	M	D				P	T	S	D
O	S	B	N				B	O	H	O
K	H	F	R	I	D	G	E	O	I	E	W
E	E	N	U	U	J	G	D	A	L	L	P
R	R	W	C	L	O	C	K	R	E	F	E
B	A	T	H	R	O	O	M	D	T	P	H

4 Word snake

Finde die unregelmäßigen simple past-Formen in der Schlange. Trage sie und ihre Infinitivformen unten ein.

AUGHTKLPOKNEWUIKOPU
TAUGHTKLPOKNEWUIKOPU
PNWORETBXYSOLDHKQXYT
THOUGHTLMUFOUNDKQP
MIULBOUGHTRESWONAED
KOPHEARDHQWCUNDERSTO

1 *heard*   *hear*

2 _____   _____

3 _____   _____

4 _____   _____

5 _____   _____

6 _____   _____

7 _____   _____

8 _____   _____

9 _____   _____

10 _____   _____

New words ▸ *p. 28*

Was ist los, Dan?

Mein neuer Pullover sieht **furchtbar** aus.

Meiner sieht auch schrecklich aus!

Jeder weiß, dass ich grün gar nicht mag.

Geh weg – ich **habe die Nase voll von** dir.

Ich **verliere** oft meine Füller und Bleistifte.

Welch ein **dummer** Fehler!

Hat deine Familie ein großes Auto, Sophie?

Ich bin fertig. – **Schön!** Dann können wir gehen.

_____ , Dan?

My new pullover looks _____ .

_____ looks terrible too!

_____ knows that I hate green.

Go away – I' _____ you.

I often _____ my pens and pencils.

What a _____ mistake!

Does your family _____ a big car, Sophie?

I'm ready. – _____ ! Then we can go.

5 Lost words

Ergänze die Sätze mit den Wörtern aus den Luftballons

1 That isn't Sophie's jacket. _Hers_ is on the chair.

2 Ananda and Dilip! Are these magazines _____ ?

3 This can't be my MP3 player – _____ is small and black.

4 That isn't Dan and Jo's ball – _____ is over there in the corner.

5 He took my phone number and gave me _____ .

6 If you haven't got a football, we can give you _____ .

mine

theirs

his

yours

ours

hers

6 The fourth word

Welches Wort fehlt hier?

1 play – theatre / film – _____

2 fly – flew / lose – _____

3 win – won / spend – _____

4 she – hers / we – _____

5 cap – head / trousers – _____

6 life – lives / shelf – _____

7 bike – ride / horse – _____

8 city – cities / country – _____

9 nothing – everything / nobody – _____

10 white – black / clever – _____

11 rabbit – hutch / parrot – _____

12 rehearse – rehearsal / build – _____

13 7 days – week / 60 minutes – _____

14 your pen – yours / my pen – _____

New words ▸ *p. 29*

Ich kann dir helfen, wenn du ein **Problem** hast.	I can help you if you've got a _____ .
Er hörte mich und **schaute auf**.	He heard me and _____ .
Ich brauche neue T-Shirts. – **Wofür**?	I need new T-shirts. – _____ ?
Meine **alten** sind zu klein.	My _____ are too small.
Dan hat **mehr** Mützen **als ich**.	Dan has got _____ caps _____ .
Jo **zeigte auf** Dan. „Mein Zwilling!" sagte er.	Jo _____ Dan. 'My twin!' he said.
Wo ist Ananda? – Ich bin nicht **sicher**.	Where is Ananda? – I'm not _____ .

7 Words with different meanings

*Finde die passenden Wörter zu den Paaren 1–10
auf den Zetteln und trage sie ein.
Unterstreiche die deutschen Entsprechungen.*

Denkt daran!
Manche Wörter haben
mehr als eine
Bedeutung

1
a) ein Leben retten
b) Geld sparen
save

6
a) ein freier Tag
b) eine kostenlose Eintrittskarte
_____

7
a) vor 8 Uhr
b) bevor ich gehe
_____

4
a) die richtige Antwort
b) auf der rechten Seite
_____

2
a) neue Leute kennenlernen
b) sich jede Woche treffen
_____

8
a) in der Gegenwart
b) ein schönes Geschenk
_____

free
look
save
cool
know
show
right
just
present
meet

9
a) ein cooles T-Shirt
b) kühles Wetter
_____

3
a) die Antwort wissen
b) nette Leute kennen
_____

5
a) eine großartige Show
b) Hausaufgaben dem Lehrer zeigen
_____

10
a) hübsch aussehen
b) aus dem Fenster schauen
_____

New words ▸ *p. 30*

Ich denke, diese Aufgabe ist **leichter**.	I think this exercise is _____ .
Haltet bitte **den Mund** und hört zu.	Please _____ and listen.
Bist du **so** alt **wie** Ananda?	Are you _____ old _____ Ananda?
Ja, und ich bin auch sehr **schlau**!	Yes, I am. And I'm very _____ too!
Du irrst dich. Oder ist es mein Fehler?	No, _____ . Or is it my mistake?
Ich **verkaufte** mein Fahrrad für 100 Pfund.	I _____ my bike for £100.

8 What are the words?

Lies die Informationen und vervollständige die Sätze.
Benutze die richtige Form eines Wortes aus der Box.

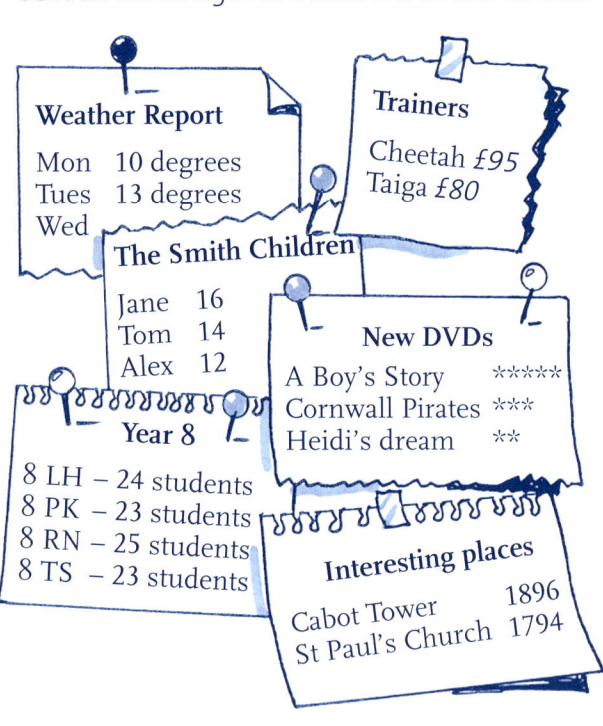

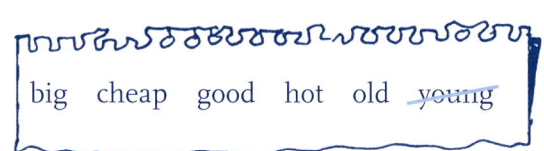

big   cheap   good   hot   old   ~~young~~

1 Alex is *the youngest* in the family.

2 Tuesday was _____ than Monday.

3 Taiga trainers are _____ than Cheetah.

4 A Boy's Story is _____ new DVD.

5 St Paul's is _____ than Cabot Tower.

6 8 RN is _____ form in Year 8.

9 Bits and pieces

Setze die Bruchstücke zusammen, um Wörter zu bilden. Übersetze sie ins Deutsche.

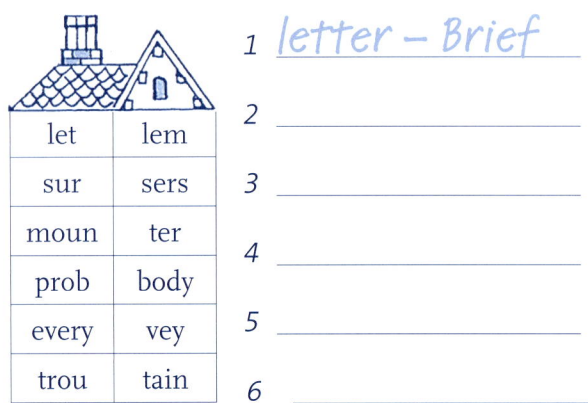

1 *letter – Brief*

2 _____

3 _____

4 _____

5 _____

6 _____

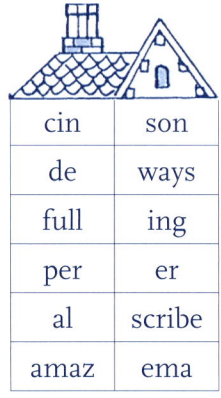

7 _____

8 _____

9 _____

10 _____

11 _____

12 _____

New words ▸ *pp. 31–37*

Es ist so warm in der Karibik, **sogar** im Winter.	It's so warm in the Caribbean, _____ in winter.
Mathe ist **langweiliger** als Geschichte.	Maths is _____ than history.
Das **langweiligste** Schulfach ist Sport.	The _____ subject is PE.
Recycling ist eine gute Sache.	_____ is a good thing.
Wir verwenden nur **recyceltes** Papier.	We only use _____ paper.
Wir warteten **ungefähr** eine Stunde.	We waited for _____ an hour.
Wie viele **Punkte** hat unsere Mannschaft?	How many _____ has our team got?
Lass uns es in einem **Kaufhaus** kaufen.	Let's buy it at a _____ .

10 Word friends

a) Ordne die Wörter auf der Wiese dem richtigen Verb zu.

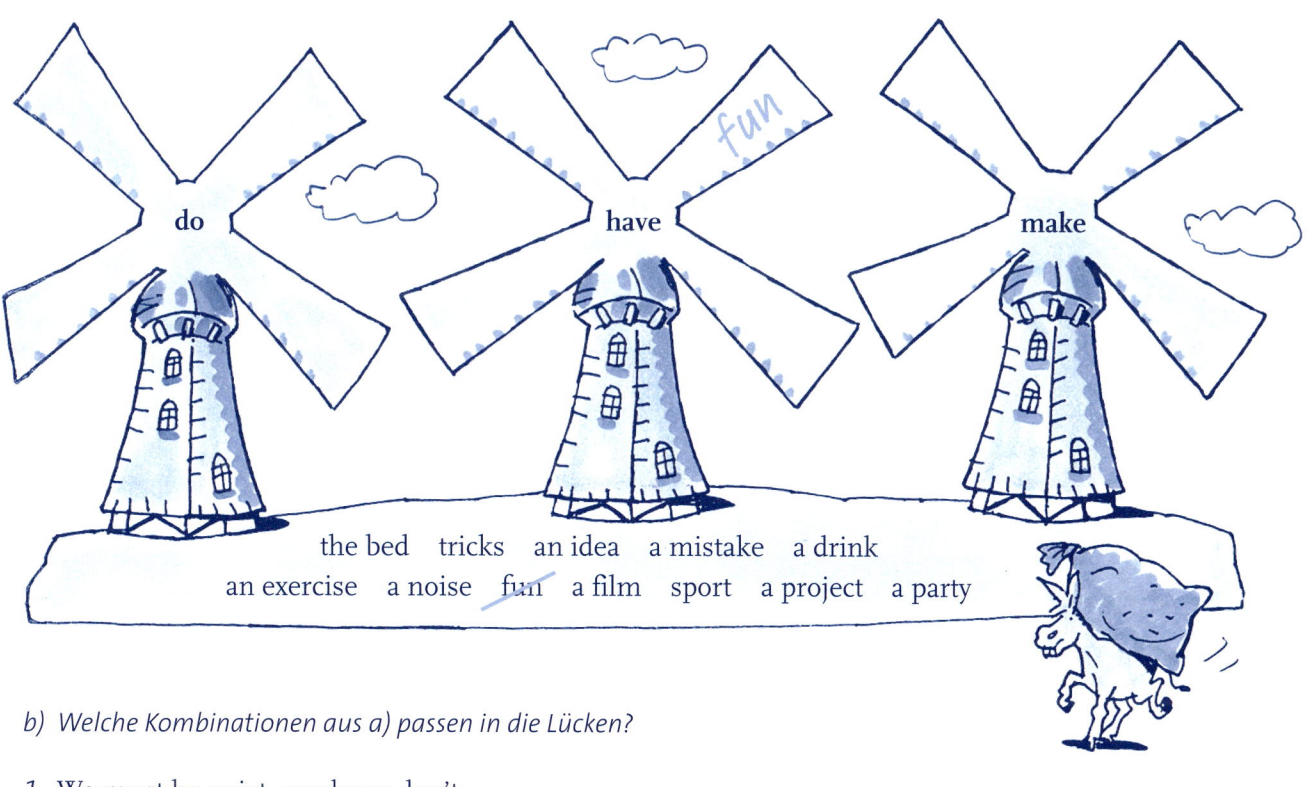

do   have   make

the bed   tricks   an idea   a mistake   a drink
an exercise   a noise   fun   a film   sport   a project   a party

b) Welche Kombinationen aus a) passen in die Lücken?

1 We must be quiet, so please don't _____ .

2 May I _____ ? – I'm very thirsty.

3 Do you _____ at school? – Yes, we play football on Wednesdays.

4 What can we do tomorrow? – I _____ ! Let's go to the cinema.

5 I'm going to John's party now. – OK. _____ , but don't be late.

6 We want to _____ on Bristol in our English class.

New words ▸ *pp. 38 – 39*

Ich las ein Buch **als** ich auf das Flugzeug wartete. I read a book _____ I waited for the plane.

Lasst uns zur **Mode**schau gehen. Let's go to the _____ show.

Wollt ihr euch uns **anschließen**? Do you want to _____ us?

Kann ich der **Moderator** sein? Can I be the _____ ?

Sophie rannte **hinüber zur** Bühne. Sophie ran _____ the stage.

Sie **liebt** Modeschauen. She _____ fashion shows.

Musik ist meine große **Liebe**. Music is my big _____ .

Sei **vorsichtig**, wenn du dieses Kleid anziehst. Be _____ when you put on this dress.

Meine Mutter **entwarf** es letztes Jahr. My mum _____ it last year.

Was hältst du von diesem **Hut**? What do you think about this _____ ?

Furchtbar! Schau einfach in den **Spiegel**. Awful! Just look in the _____ .

Gibt es keinen Stuhl? Ich möchte nicht **stehen**. Isn't there a chair? I don't want to _____ .

Ich brauche dieses **Zeug** nicht. Wirf es weg! I don't need this _____ . Throw it away!

Bitte **beeile dich**! Die Show beginnt. Please _____ ! The show is starting.

Jo fiel vom Bett und **landete** auf dem Fußboden. Jo fell off the bed and _____ on the floor.

Wie kann ich mich **auf** den Test **vorbereiten**? How can I _____ the test?

Dan war **verwirrt**. Warum war Jo nicht zu Hause? Dan was _____ . Why wasn't Jo at home?

Bitte wirf die alten Sachen in die **Mülltonne**. Please throw the old things in the _____ .

11 Opposites

Trage die Gegenteile der fett gedruckten Wörter in die Lücken ein.

1 a **white** / *black* cat

2 We **hate** / _____ school.

3 the **best** / _____ essay

4 a **small** / _____ house

5 **expensive** / _____ clothes

6 We **lost** / _____ the match.

7 I **lost** / _____ some money.

8 **boring** / _____ lessons

9 **before** / _____ breakfast

10 a **slow**/ _____ train

11 at the **bottom** of / at the _____ of the page

12 in the **foreground** / in the _____

12 Pronunciation

Vervollständige die Listen mit Wörtern aus der Box.
In jeder Liste müssen sich die Wörter reimen.

Markiere für jede Liste das passende Lautschriftsymbol.

design flew mine one
pair prepare shine sun
there threw through won

1		2		3		4	
one	aɪ	fair	aɪ	_____	aɪ	_____	aɪ
run	(ʌ)	_____	ʌ	fine	ʌ	_____	ʌ
_____	eə	_____	eə	_____	eə	_____	eə
_____	uː	_____	uː	_____	uː	who	uː

Ordne die Lautschrift dem Wort zu.

1	'kʌntri	bunk	4	'steəz	stairs	7	dɪ'skraɪb	describe	10	ruːd	cool
2	sʌn	country	5	skeəd	careful	8	aɪ	island	11	kuːl	ruler
3	bʌŋk	son	6	'keəfl	scared	9	'aɪlənd	eye	12	'ruːlə	rude

Ordne die englischen Wörter der Lautschrift zu,
um den geheimen Satz zu finden.

the where on be
always an like I'd
to shines island – sun

aɪd   laɪk   tə   biː   ɒn   ən   -'aɪlənd   weə   ðə   sʌn

'ɔːlweɪz   ʃaɪnz   .

13 Word groups

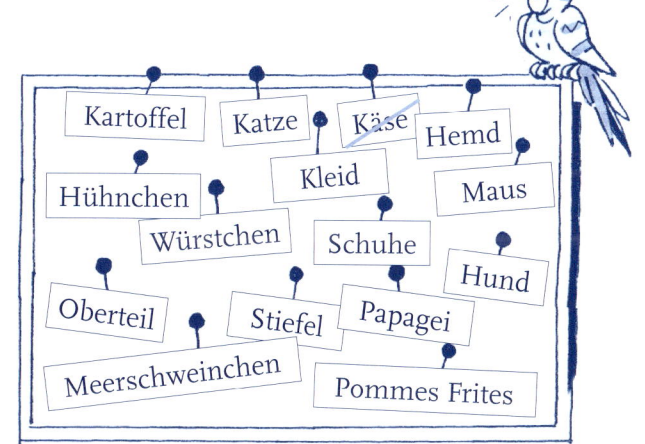

Übersetze die deutschen Wörter in der Box ins Englische
und füge sie in die richtige Wortgruppe ein.

food	clothes	pets
cheese		

Kartoffel Katze Käse Hemd
Hühnchen Kleid Maus
Würstchen Schuhe
Oberteil Stiefel Papagei Hund
Meerschweinchen Pommes Frites

Unit 3

New words ▸ *pp. 42 – 43*

Heute sprechen wir über **Tiere**.	Today we are talking about _____ .
Füchse sind sehr schlau.	_____ are very clever.
Lass uns die **Sendereihe** über Tiere gucken.	Let's watch this _____ about animals.
Geht es um **wilde** Tiere?	Is it about _____ animals?
Manche Tiere **überleben** den Winter nicht.	Some animals don't _____ the winter.
Von hier kannst du manchmal **Rehe** sehen.	From here you can sometimes see _____ .
Kannst du auch die **Spechte** hören?	Can you hear the _____ too?
Ist der Vogel rot oder **grau**?	Is the bird red or _____ ?
Schau, dort drüben ist ein **Eichhörnchen**!	Look, there's a _____ over there!
Hilfe! Wir haben einen **Maulwurf** im Garten.	Help! We've got a _____ in our garden.
Nein, ich glaube es ist ein **Igel**.	No, I think it's a _____ .
Es sind viele **Frösche** in der Nähe des Sees.	There are lots of _____ near the lake.

1 Scrambled words: pets

Welche Tiere sind das?
Die markierten Buchstaben ergeben ein weiteres Tier.

1 gaeuin gip   g u i n e a   p i g

2 rabtib   _ _ _ _ _ _

3 sifh   _ _ _ _

4 toeiorst   _ _ _ _ _ _ _ _

5 heros   _ _ _ _ _

6 odg   _ _ _

7 bueigd   _ _ _ _ _ _

8 haremts   _ _ _ _ _ _ _

The 'secret pet' is a _____

2 Word search: wild animals

Finde sieben Tiere. Übersetze sie ins Deutsche. ( )

H	I	W	W	W	V
E	S	R	F	O	X
D	Q	F	R	O	G
G	U	M	G	D	Y
E	I	O	L	P	E
H	R	L	B	E	E
O	R	E	U	C	M
G	E	J	B	K	R
R	L	O	E	E	P
S	D	E	E	R	D

fox – Fuchs

_____

_____

_____

_____

_____

New words ▸ p. 44

Tu bitte den **Müll** in die Mülltonne.	Please put the _____ into the bin.
Du **wirst frieren** ohne Pullover.	You'_____ without a pullover.
Es ist aber warm – ich **werde nicht frieren**.	But it's warm – I _____ .
Jo ist **wahrscheinlich** auf dem **Hof**.	Jo is _____ in the _____ .
Bitte vergiss nicht Sophie **anzumailen**.	Please don't forget to _____ Sophie.
Wir sollten **uns hinsetzen** und darüber sprechen.	Let's _____ and talk about it.
Wann kannst du mir den Brief **schicken**?	When can you _____ me the letter?
Kannst du den **Mond** hinter den Wolken sehen?	Can you see the _____ behind the clouds?

3 Word snail

*Trage die simple past-Formen der angegebenen
deutschen Wörter in die Schnecke ein.
Die Anfangsbuchstaben in der Schnecke
helfen dir.*

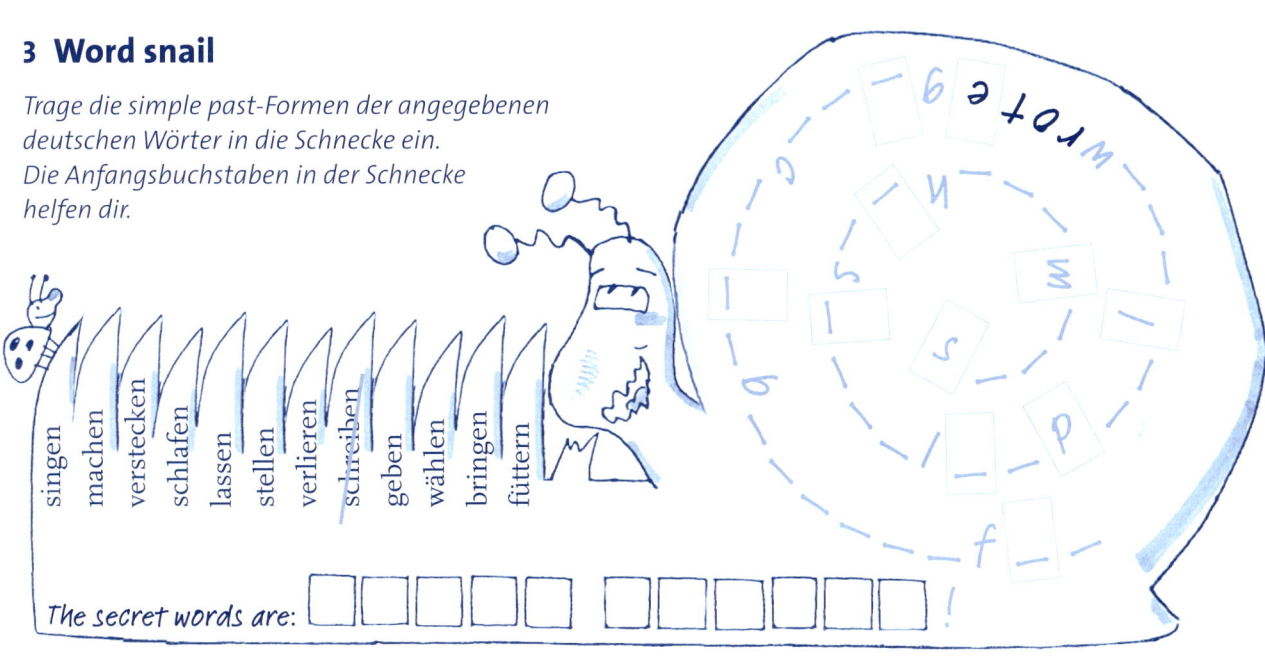

singen · machen · verstecken · schlafen · lassen · stellen · verlieren · schreiben · geben · wählen · bringen · füttern

The secret words are: ☐☐☐☐☐ ☐☐☐☐☐☐ !

4 Word ladder

Gehe von unten nach oben, indem du bei jeder Sprosse einen Buchstaben veränderst.

find

lost

most

Where's my key? I can't ★ it.

Is the weather OK? – Yes, it's ★.

A foot has got ★ toes.

Dan and Jo ★ in Bristol.

'★' is the opposite of 'hate'.

Here's the money. Don't ★ it!

I ★ my mobile yesterday, but I found it again.

★ people are happy when the sun shines.

New words ▸ *p. 45*

Vielen Dank für deine Hilfe.   _____ for your help.

Ruf mich an, **falls** du mich nochmals brauchst.   Call me _____ you need me again.

Sophie ist **krank.** Sie bleibt heute im Bett.   Sophie's _____ . She's staying in bed today.

Englisch ist eine sehr **wichtige** Sprache.   English is a very _____ language.

Wie kann ich meine Füße warm **halten**?   How can I _____ my feet warm?

Morgen wird es dir wieder **gut**gehen.   You'll be _____ again tomorrow.

Das Buch liegt auf dem Boden. **Heb** es bitte **auf.**   The book is on the floor. Please _____ it _____ .

5 Definitions

Vervollständige die Definitionen mit Wörtern von der Tafel.
Trage die richtigen Wörter aus den Seifenblasen in die rechte Spalte ein.

Blackboard words: bin   building   ~~grey~~   night   ready   shines   shoes   sport   throw   trees   watch   word

Bubble words: cinema   moon   rubbish   prepare   trainers   ~~squirrel~~

1 This animal is red or *grey* and lives in _____ .   *squirrel*

2 You can wear these _____ when you do _____ .   _____

3 You often see this in the sky at _____ – it _____ .   _____

4 In this _____ you can _____ films.   _____

5 You don't want this, so you _____ it in the _____ .   _____

6 This is another _____ for 'get _____'.   _____

6 Odd word out

Ein Wort passt nicht. Finde und unterstreiche es.

1 squirrel – hedgehog – grey – mole

2 sleep – brought – fed – wrote

3 today – holiday – yesterday – tomorrow

4 best – bigger – biggest – smallest

5 trousers – shirt – jacket – person

6 frog – fox – yard – woodpecker

New words ▸ p. 46

Ich verstehe es nicht. **Erkläre** es mir!　　I don't understand it. _____ it to me!

Das ist eine wirklich gute **Erklärung**.　　That's a really good _____ .

Es war ein **grauenhafter** Tag – kalt und regnerisch.　　It was a _____ day – cold and rainy.

In der **Garage** ist das Auto es **sicher**.　　The car is _____ in the _____ .

7 The fourth word

Welches Wort fehlt hier?

1 pencil – pencil case / rubbish – _____

2 day – sun / night – _____

3 rabbit – hutch / car – _____

4 is – isn't / will be – _____

5 four – number / grey – _____

6 invite – invitation / explain – _____

8 Numbers and letters

Zu jeder Zahl gehört ein Buchstabe. Finde die Lösungswörter und dann den „geheimen Satz".

1 Please speak $\underset{10}{S}$ $\underset{1}{\ }$ $\underset{5}{\ }$ $\underset{14}{\ }$ $\underset{1}{\ }$ $\underset{6}{\ }$ and $\underset{13}{\ }$ $\underset{1}{\ }$ $\underset{18}{\ }$ $\underset{3}{\ }$ $\underset{11}{R}$ $\underset{1}{\ }$ $\underset{6}{\ }$

2 Sophie shouted $\underset{3}{\ }$ $\underset{9}{\ }$ $\underset{4}{\ }$ $\underset{11}{\ }$ $\underset{8}{\ }$ $\underset{1}{\ }$ $\underset{6}{\ }$ at Dilip.

3 Dan and Jo called their dad and he came $\underset{12}{\ }$ $\underset{2}{\ }$ $\underset{8}{\ }$ $\underset{13}{\ }$ $\underset{15}{\ }$ $\underset{1}{\ }$ $\underset{6}{\ }$.

4 The children played $\underset{16}{\ }$ $\underset{3}{\ }$ $\underset{20}{\ }$ $\underset{20}{\ }$ $\underset{8}{\ }$ $\underset{1}{\ }$ $\underset{6}{\ }$ on the beach.

5 Ananda, please listen very $\underset{13}{C}$ $\underset{3}{\ }$ $\underset{11}{\ }$ $\underset{18}{\ }$ $\underset{19}{\ }$ $\underset{2}{\ }$ $\underset{1}{\ }$ $\underset{1}{\ }$ $\underset{6}{\ }$.

6 Jack waited $\underset{9}{\ }$ $\underset{18}{\ }$ $\underset{11}{\ }$ $\underset{7}{\ }$ $\underset{5}{\ }$ $\underset{2}{\ }$ $\underset{10}{\ }$ $\underset{1}{\ }$ $\underset{6}{\ }$ in front of Mr Kingsley's room.

7 Boys and girls, please don't sing this song so $\underset{1}{\ }$ $\underset{5}{\ }$ $\underset{2}{\ }$ $\underset{17}{D}$ $\underset{1}{\ }$ $\underset{6}{\ }$.

The secret sentence is:

$\underset{17}{\ }$ $\underset{3}{\ }$ $\underset{17}{\ }$ $\quad$ $\underset{3}{\ }$ $\underset{1}{\ }$ $\underset{14}{\ }$ $\underset{3}{\ }$ $\underset{6}{\ }$ $\underset{10}{\ }$ $\quad$ $\underset{17}{\ }$ $\underset{11}{\ }$ $\underset{8}{\ }$ $\underset{7}{\ }$ $\underset{18}{\ }$ $\underset{10}{\ }$ $\quad$ $\underset{10}{\ }$ $\underset{1}{\ }$ $\underset{5}{\ }$ $\underset{14}{\ }$ $\underset{1}{\ }$ $\underset{6}{\ }$ $\quad$ $\underset{3}{\ }$ $\underset{9}{\ }$ $\underset{17}{\ }$

$\underset{13}{\ }$ $\underset{3}{\ }$ $\underset{11}{\ }$ $\underset{18}{\ }$ $\underset{19}{\ }$ $\underset{2}{\ }$ $\underset{1}{\ }$ $\underset{1}{\ }$ $\underset{6}{\ }$ $\quad$ $\underset{5}{\ }$ $\underset{9}{\ }$ $\quad$ $\underset{11}{\ }$ $\underset{3}{\ }$ $\underset{8}{\ }$ $\underset{9}{\ }$ $\underset{6}{\ }$ $\quad$ $\underset{17}{\ }$ $\underset{3}{\ }$ $\underset{6}{\ }$ $\underset{10}{\ }$.

New words ▸ *pp. 47 – 52*

Ananda, du hast wirklich **gute Arbeit** geleistet.   Ananda, you did a really _____ .

Ich gehe jetzt zur Tier**klinik**.   I'm going to the animal _____ now.

Ich kann sehr **gut** Englisch sprechen.   I can speak English very _____ .

Mein Handy ist **kaputt**. Ich brauche ein neues.   My mobile is _____ I need a new one.

Wird es eine **schwere** Arbeit sein?   Will it be _____ work?

Ich möchte heute nicht **hart arbeiten**.   I don't want to _____ today.

Leider brauche ich deine Hilfe.   I need your help, _____ .

Haben diese Tiere **Feinde**?   Do these animals have _____ ?

Er **suchte** die Liste **ab**, um seinen Namen zu finden.   He _____ the list to find his name.

Mutti **bekam** letzten Monat **ein Baby**.   Last month mum _____ .

Die meisten Tiere haben Angst vor **Feuer**.   Most animals are afraid of _____ .

Sie **schlug ihm** auf den Kopf.   She _____ on the head.

Dies ist eine Übung zur **Wortbildung**.   This is an exercise on _____ .

Warum ist dieser Ort so **berühmt**?   Why is this place so _____ ?

Kann ich bitte Ihre **Adresse** haben?   Can I have your _____ please?

9 Picture puzzle

Welche Tiere erkennst du in der Zeichnung?

_____

_____

_____

_____

_____

_____

10 Spot the mistakes

In jedem Satz sind zwei Fehler. Unterstreiche und korrigiere sie.

1 There's a new <u>serie</u> of five programes about wild animals.   *series* _____

2 Their are more wild animals in the city then people think.   _____ _____

3 We don't see fokses very often in citys because they don't like us.   _____ _____

4 Ananda saw too baby hedgehogs near the dastbin.   _____ _____

5 Milk is not well for hedgehogs. They wants water.   _____ _____

11 Word groups

Übersetze die Wörter auf der Wiese. Schreibe die englischen Wörter in die passende Seifenblase.

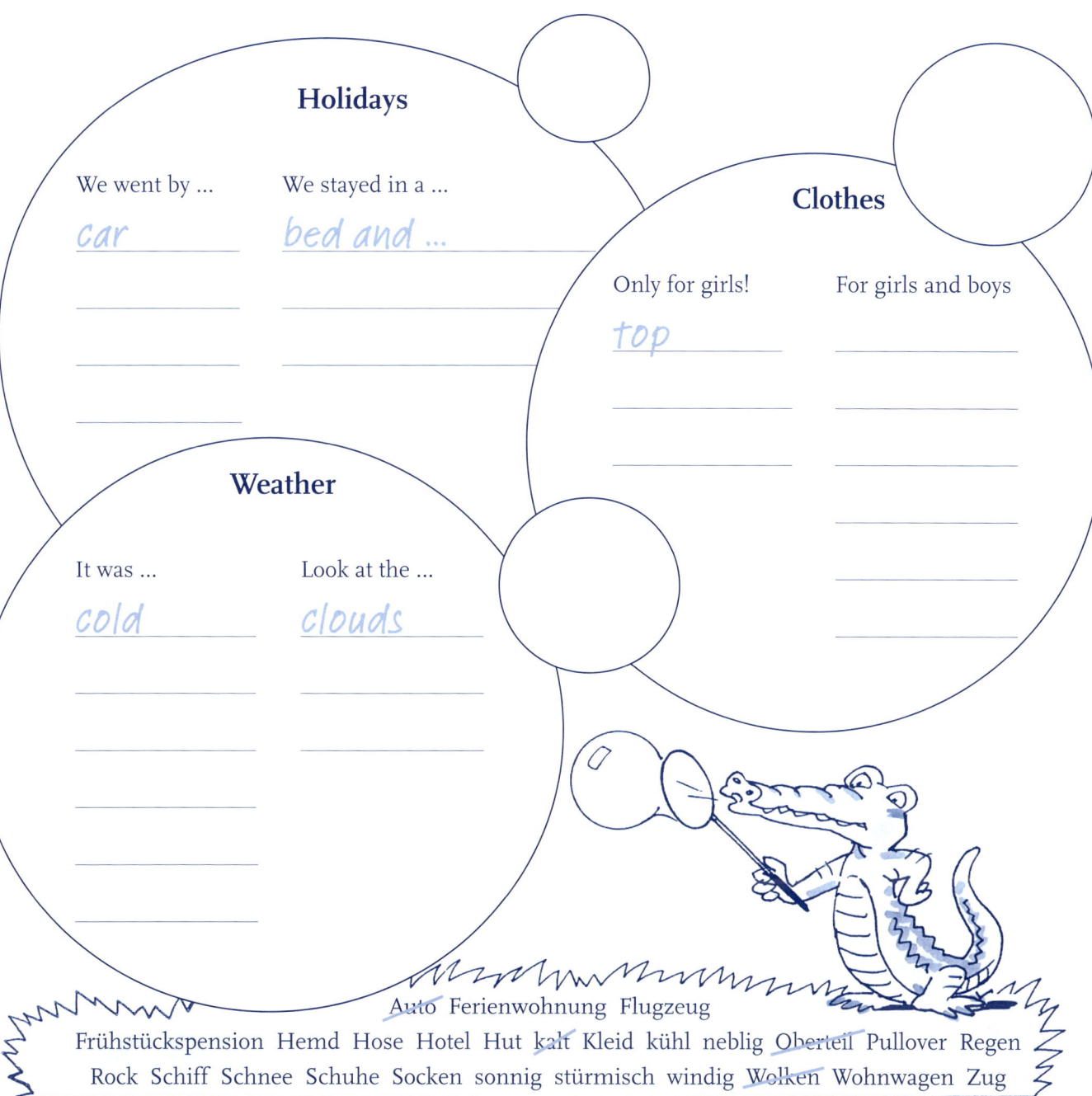

Holidays

We went by ...
car

We stayed in a ...
bed and ...

Clothes

Only for girls!
top

For girls and boys

Weather

It was ...
cold

Look at the ...
clouds

Auto Ferienwohnung Flugzeug
Frühstückspension Hemd Hose Hotel Hut kalt Kleid kühl neblig Oberteil Pullover Regen
Rock Schiff Schnee Schuhe Socken sonnig stürmisch windig Wolken Wohnwagen Zug

New words ▸ *pp. 54 – 55*

Mike ist wirklich kein **Engel**.	Mike really is no _____ .
Er **tyrannisiert** jüngere Schüler.	He _____ younger students.
Weißt du, wo mein **Koffer** ist?	Do you know where my _____ is?
Ich muss jetzt **packen**.	I have to _____ now.
Der Zug **fährt** um 8.30 Uhr nach London **ab**.	The train _____ for London at 8.30.
Tim **verließ** das Zimmer und ging weg.	Tim _____ the room and went away.
Er **ließ** seine Tasche auf dem Tisch **zurück**.	He _____ his bag on the table.
Mein Hamster **sprang** aus dem Fenster.	My hamster _____ out of the window.
Ich werde den Hamster wirklich **vermissen**.	I'll really _____ the hamster.
Ich **versprach**, mein Zimmer aufzuräumen.	I _____ to tidy my room.
Jetzt ist alles **schön ordentlich**.	Everything is _____ now.
Jack sieht in seiner Uniform sehr **gepflegt** aus.	Jack looks very _____ in his uniform.
Und sein Zimmer sieht sehr **aufgeräumt** aus.	And his room looks very _____ .
Sei ein **Schatz** und räum dein Zimmer auf.	Be a _____ and tidy your room.
Ich bin so traurig – mein **Herz** ist gebrochen.	I'm so sad – my _____ is broken.
Wir müssen aus dieser Wohnung **ausziehen**.	We have to _____ of this flat.
Warum **zieht** ihr nicht **nach** London?	Why don't you _____ London?
Jo ist **schon** hier.	Jo is _____ here.
Bitte kauft euch eine **Rückfahrkarte**.	Please buy a _____ .
Zählt mal euer Geld bitte.	_____ your money please.
Oje, wir haben kein Geld.	_____ , we haven't got any money.
Du darfst auch hingehen – wenn du **brav** bist!	You can go too – if you're _____ !
Sophie **drehte sich um**, um mich anzuschauen.	Sophie _____ to look at me.
Sie ist ein sehr **schüchternes** Mädchen.	She's a very _____ girl.
Kannst du das neue Wort in **Zeile** 14 erklären?	Can you explain the new word in _____ 14?
Ich will einen **Brief** an Sophie schreiben.	I want to write a _____ to Sophie.
Am Wochenende **fühle** ich mich immer good.	I always _____ good at weekends.

12 Crossword

Across

1 a 'hotel' behind your car (7)
3 simple past of 'speak' (5)
5 Ananda can't go to school today because she's ★. (3)
6 sit – sat / stand – ★ (5)
8 Lots of people need them to see better. (7)
9 opposite of 'friend' (5)
10 You'll get 5 ★ for the right answer. (6)
12 opposite of 'fast' (4)
13 I ate biscuits and ★ milk. (5)
17 opposite of 'hate' (4)
18 After he got up Jack ★ the table for breakfast. (4)
20 take photos / ★ sport (2)
21 Germany, France and Britain are European ★. (9)
22 You put rubbish in it. (7)
26 cloud – cloudy / rain – ★ (5)

27 simple past of 'wear' (4)
28 opposite of 'boring' (8)
32 simple past of 'feel' (4)
33 Have you got a book ★ English dogs? (5)
34 do – did / buy – ★ (6)
35 a small green animal that can jump well (4)
36 60 minutes = 1 ★ (4)
37 a house for cars (6)
38 a place where you can see films (6)
39 Your room is always so neat and ★. (4)

Down

1 opposite of 'expensive' (5)
2 you – yours / me – ★ (4)
3 opposite of 'big' (5)
4 Jo didn't know the answer, but Dan ★ it. (4)
7 plural of 'deer' (4)

11 I ★ about the problem and then I found an answer. (7)
12 I'm sure the sun will ★ today. (5)
13 noun – description / verb – ★ (8)
14 very bad, terrible (5)
15 something – somebody / nothing – ★ (6)
16 simple past of 'find' (5)
19 The cupboard is empty – there's ★ in it. (7)
23 simple past of 'see' (3)
24 simple past of 'eat' (3)
25 verb – fly / noun – ★ (6)
29 opposite of 'before' (5)
30 simple past of 'choose' (5)
31 American English: elevator / British English: ★ (4)
32 You can't see very far on a ★ day. (5)
36 You wear it on your head. (3)

Unit 4

New words ▸ p. 58 – 59

Dieses Dorf ist sehr **sauber**.	This village is very _____ .
Und es gibt so viele **Kühe** hier.	And there are so many _____ here.
Einige Städte sind so **schmutzig**!	Some cities are so _____ !
Oft gibt es viele **Fabriken** dort.	There are often lots of _____ there.
Unsere Freunde leben auf einem **Bauernhof**.	Our friends live on a _____ .
Jetzt spielen sie **auf dem Feld**.	Now they're playing _____ .
Ein Spaziergang im **Wald** ist auch schön.	A walk in the _____ is nice too.
Die **Hügel** sind nicht weit von hier.	The _____ aren't far from here.
In London ist viel **Verkehr**.	There's lots of _____ in London.
Deshalb ist es immer so **laut**.	That's why it's always so _____ .
Können wir in diesem **Fluss** schwimmen?	Can we swim in this _____ ?
Schaut die **Schafe** im **Tal** an.	Look at the _____ in the _____ .
Dan kann seinen **Schlafanzug** nicht finden.	Dan can't find his _____ .

1 What's the word: *in* or *on*?

*Füge **on** oder **in** in die Lücken ein.*
Trage die passende deutsche
Präposition in dieTabelle ein.

Hey Wordmaster ...
in the kitchen heißt doch *in der Küche*
aber *in the field* heißt *auf dem Feld*.
Sehr witzig!

Ja, Ken.
Präpositionen sind
schwer! So
hilft es oft, wenn
du Präposition und
Nomen zusammen
lernst.

1 We live _____*in*_____ a big city.   _____*in*_____ einer großen Stadt

2 But our friends live _____ the country.   _____ dem Land

3 Can you write it _____ the board, please?   _____ die Tafel

4 The twins are _____ the train now.   _____ Zug

5 Look at all those clouds _____ the sky.   _____ Himmel

6 Ananda is talking to Sophie _____*on*_____ the phone.   _____*am*_____ Telefon

7 It's raining now, but we can meet _____ the afternoon.   _____ Nachmittag

8 Let's listen to the weather report _____ the radio.   _____ Radio

New words ▸ *p. 60*

Die Pizza **riecht** großartig.	The pizza _____ great.
Papa ist in der Küche. Er **kocht** gerade.	Dad's in the kitchen. He's _____ .
Gestern hatten wir **walisisches** Essen.	Yesterday we had _____ food.
Die **Suppe** war sehr gut.	The _____ was very good.
Lass uns ins **Eisenbahn**museum gehen.	Let's go to the _____ museum.
Gibt es noch andere **Sehenswürdigkeiten** hier?	Are there any other _____ here?
Das **Schloss** ist sehr interessant.	The _____ is very interesting.
Ich habe keine Angst vor **Geistern**.	I'm not afraid of _____ .
Bitte lest auch diesen **Absatz**.	Please read this _____ too.

2 Word families

Vervollständige die Tabelle. Benutze dann fünf Wörter aus der fertigen Tabelle, um die Sätze zu ergänzen.

Verb	visit			describe	answer		paint
Noun	*visit*	explanation	flight			glue	

1 Can you _____ this word, please? I don't understand it.

2 Do you remember your first _____ to a museum?

3 Do you want to _____ to London? Or is it faster to go by train?

4 I really like his pictures. He's a fantastic _____ .

5 The old woman gave the police a very good _____ of the bank robber.

3 Odd word out

Ein Wort passt nicht. Finde und unterstreiche es.

1 hamburger – pizza – picnic – soup

2 smell – hear – see – paint

3 river – tower – bridge – castle

4 Welsh – French – Germany – English

5 soup – chicken – potatoes – cook

6 paragraph – sights – word – sentence

7 chicken – farm – cow – sheep

8 rhino – hippo – camel – woodpecker

9 kitchen – bathroom – hall – yard

10 noise – awful – horrible – terrible

11 clean – dirty – neat – tidy

12 mountain – river – lake – sea

New words ▶ p. 61

Möchtest du etwas **Schinkenspeck**?	Would you like some _____ ?
Ja, und ich möchte auch **Eier**.	Yes, and I'd like some _____ too.
Hast du den neuen **Fahrplan**?	Have you got the new _____ ?
Ich habe **gerade** Sandwiches **gemacht**.	I've _____ sandwiches.
Du kannst auch ein Stück **Pastete** haben.	You can have a piece of _____ too.
Hast du mein Mäppchen **gesehen**?	Have you _____ my pencil case?
Papa ist gerade nach Hause **gekommen**.	Dad has just _____ home.
Wie geht es Tante Anne? Es geht ihr **gut**, danke.	How's Aunt Anne? She's _____ , thank you.

4 Word snake

Finde zehn Infinitive in der Wortschlange und ergänze die fehlenden Formen.

1 be   was   been   6 _____

2 _____   7 _____

3 _____   8 _____

4 _____   9 _____

5 _____   10 _____

5 Word friends

Welche Wörter passen zu dem, was die Maus gerade denkt? Finde für jede Maus die zwei richigen Käsestücke.

6 The fourth word

Welches Wort fehlt hier?

1 bad – good / dirty – _____

2 food – feed / interview – _____

3 word – sentence / sentence – _____

4 slow – fast / quiet – _____

5 eyes – see / nose – _____

6 do – done / take – _____

7 cow – cows / sheep – _____

8 England – English / Wales – _____

7 Word mix

Bringe die Wörter in die richtige Reihenfolge.

1 Wales. on go holiday to Let's   *Let's go on holiday to Wales.*

2 are There old lots there. castles of   _____

3 mountains, and You'll see valleys. hills   _____

4 an place. interesting The railway is museum.   _____

5 Welsh Welsh. people speak Many   _____

6 speaks too. everybody English But   _____

7 the language! have So won't we problems with   _____

8 Hour glasses

Übersetze die Wörter und trage sie in die passende Sanduhr ein.

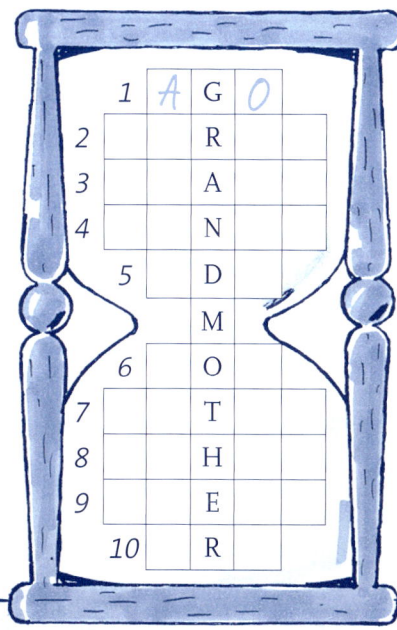

1 ~~vor~~ – Bett

2 sich einigen - Füchse

3 leer – Strand

4 Salat – witzig, komisch

5 schlecht, schlimm –
    hinzufügen, ergänzen

6 Hund – war

7 beobachten – hasste

8 andere(r,s) – Geräusch, Lärm

9 Fußboden – Pause

10 Ende, Schluss – sind

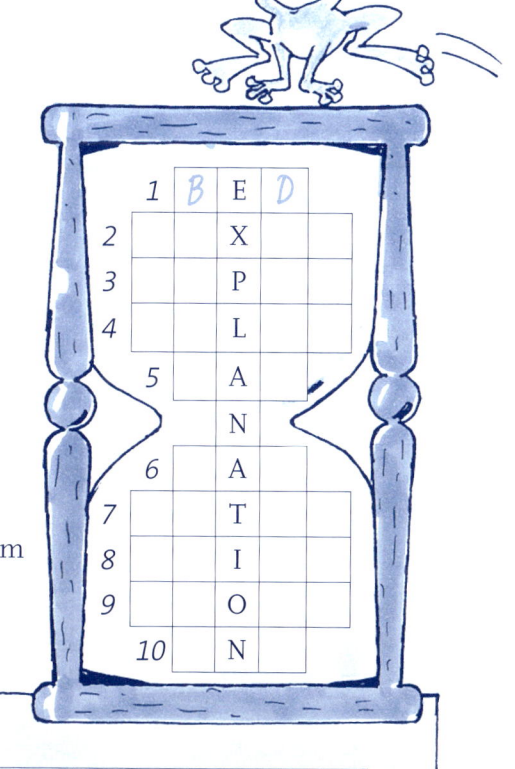

Left hourglass vertical word: **GRANDMOTHER**
(1 A G O, 2 R, 3 A, 4 N, 5 D, M, 6 O T, 7 H, 8 E, 9 R, 10)

Right hourglass vertical word: **EXPLANATION**
(1 B E D, 2 X, 3 P, 4 L, 5 A, N, 6 A T, 7 I, 8 O, 9 N, 10)

Die senkrechten Wörter in den Sanduhren heißen: links _____

                  rechts _____

New words ▸ *p. 62*

Ich habe **Kopfschmerzen**.	I have _____ .
Kannst du deine Zehen **berühren**?	Can you _____ your toes?
Hat Dan **Fieber**?	Does Dan _____ ?
Die **Temperatur** heute ist ungefähr 19°.	The _____ today is about 19°.
Jo, kannst du das **Thermometer** holen?	Jo, can you get the _____ ?
Dan hat auch **Halsschmerzen**.	Dan has got _____ too.
Trink etwas Tee – er ist gut für deinen **Hals**.	Have some tea – it's good for your _____ .
Kannst du **mit dem** Kopf **nicken**?	Can you _____ head?
Bitte **bewege** dich jetzt nicht.	Please don't _____ now.
Die **Sanitäter** sind schon hier.	The _____ are already here.

9 Word search: parts of the body

Finde 18 Wörter, die im Rätsel versteckt sind, und dann das geheime Wort. (   )

_____

arm

_____

_____

_____

_____

_____

P	C	A	P	F	U	B	T	O	E	S
A	A	R	E	O	H	F	K	K	A	T
W	T	M	J	O	Y	I	N	J	R	O
S	O	T	U	T	V	N	E	H	X	M
H	O	F	A	C	E	G	E	H	Y	A
O	T	N	T	I	C	E	E	Y	E	C
U	H	O	H	A	M	R	Y	X	R	H
L	E	G	R	N	O	S	E	R	G	D
D	A	H	O	F	U	S	H	A	N	D
E	R	E	A	S	T	M	H	A	I	R
R	T	O	T	Q	H	E	A	D	O	Q

_____

_____

_____

_____

_____

_____

The secret word:

T _ _ _ M _ _ _ _ R

New words ▸ *pp. 63 – 65*

Hast du **jemals** einen Computer benutzt?	Have you _____ used a computer?
Ja, aber ich kann keine Software **installieren**.	Yes, but I can't _____ software.
Ist dies die Seite mit der **Anleitung**?	Is this the page with the _____ ?
Auf Seite 10 **steht**, dass ich die Maus brauche.	It _____ on page 10 that I need the mouse.
Ja, du musst auf „Installieren" **klicken**.	Yes, you have to _____ on 'install'.
Wieviel Uhr ist es **übrigens**?	What time is it _____ ?
„K" in „know" ist ein **stummer Buchstabe**.	'K' in 'know' is a _____ .
Kannst du seinen walisischen **Akzent** verstehen?	Can you understand his Welsh _____ ?

10 Lost words

Ergänze die Sätze mit den Wörtern aus den Luftballons.

1 Are you new here? I've *never* seen you before.

2 We've been to London, but we haven't been to Wales _____ .

3 I play football, but I've _____ played badminton.

4 Sorry, Jo isn't here. Oh, wait … he's _____ come through the door.

5 Jack, tidy your room now, please. I've _____ asked you three times.

6 Have you seen the new film _____ ? It's really very good.

7 Have you _____ visited the railway museum?

(balloons: already, yet, ever, just, yet, never, never)

11 Word pairs

Welche Wörter passen zusammen?

(balloons: report, software, animals, install, bike, head, dinner, pyjamas, suitcase)

nod
install
cook
pack
feed
wear
ride
write

New words ▸ *pp. 70 – 71*

Dein Handy **klingelt** gerade!	Your mobile is _____ !
Wie passierte der **Unfall**?	How did the _____ happen?
Er fuhr **ziemlich** schnell.	He was driving _____ fast.
Zieh bitte deine Jacke **an**, bevor du gehst.	Please _____ your jacket before you go.
Zieh deine Stiefel **aus** bevor du hineinkommst!	_____ your boots before you come in!
Wir waren auf der falschen Straßen**seite**.	We were on the wrong _____ of the road.
Öffnet bitte euer Bücher auf **Seite** 70.	Open your books at _____ 70. please.
Ein **Polizist** hielt uns an.	A _____ stopped us.
Eine **Polizistin** stellte Fragen.	A _____ asked questions.
Kennst du den **Fahrer**?	Do you know the _____ ?
Ist er zu schnell **gefahren**?	Did he _____ too fast?
Ist jemand **verletzt**?	Is anybody _____ ?
Tut dein Bein **weh**?	Does your leg _____ ?
Die **Feuerwehrmänner** werden dir helfen.	The _____ will help you.
Ich sah auch eine **Feuerwehrfrau**.	I saw a _____ too.
Wie schnell kannst du hundert **Meter** laufen?	How fast can you run a hundred _____ ?
Bin ich **stark** genug?	Am I _____ enough?
Oder bin ich zu **schwach**?	Or am I too _____ ?
Was **hälst** du **von** Jo? Ist er in Ordnung?	What do you _____ Jo? Is he OK?
Gestern **fiel** ein Mann in den Fluss.	A man _____ into the river yesterday.
Der **Ehemann** von Frau Kapoor ist aus Uganda.	Mrs Kapoor's _____ is from Uganda.
Herr Kapoor ruft gerade seine **Ehefrau** an.	Mr Kapoor is phoning his _____ .
Kannst du den **Rettungshubschrauber** sehen?	Can you see the _____ ?
Bist du schon mal im **Krankenhaus** gewesen?	Have you ever been in _____ ?
Hoffen wir, dass wir ihn finden.	Let's _____ that we can find him.
Bitte lass mich deine Hand **halten**.	Please let me _____ your hand.
Das war knapp!	_____ .

12 Pronunciation

Vervollständige die Listen mit Wörtern aus der Box.
In jeder Liste müssen sich die Wörter reimen.

Markiere für jede Liste das passende Lautschriftsymbol.

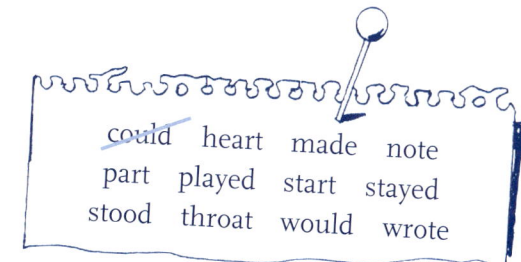

could   heart   made   note
part   played   start   stayed
stood   throat   would   wrote

could ⓤ	art ʊ	afraid ʊ	boat ʊ
good əʊ	_____ əʊ	_____ əʊ	_____ əʊ
_____ ɑː	_____ ɑː	_____ ɑː	_____ ɑː
_____ eɪ	_____ eɪ	_____ eɪ	_____ eɪ

Ordne die Lautschrift dem Wort zu.

1 kʊk	woman	4 ɑː	chance	7 greɪ	grey	10 'ʃəʊlə	alone
2 fʊt	cook	5 tʃɑːns	laugh	8 ɪk'spleɪn	wave	11 kəʊld	shoulder
3 'wʊmən	foot	6 lɑːf	are	9 weɪv	explain	12 ə'ləʊn	cold

Ordne die englischen Wörter der Lautschrift zu,
um den geheimen Satz zu finden.

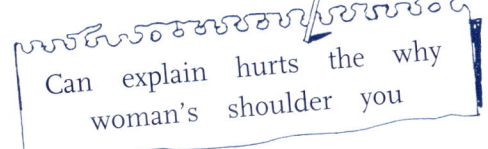

Can   explain   hurts   the   why
woman's   shoulder   you

_____ _____ _____ _____ ___ _____ _____ _____ ?
kən   juː   ɪk'spleɪn   waɪ   ðə   wʊmənz   'ʃəʊldə   hɜːts

13 Word ladder

Gehe von unten nach oben, indem du bei jeder Sprosse einen Buchstaben veränderst.

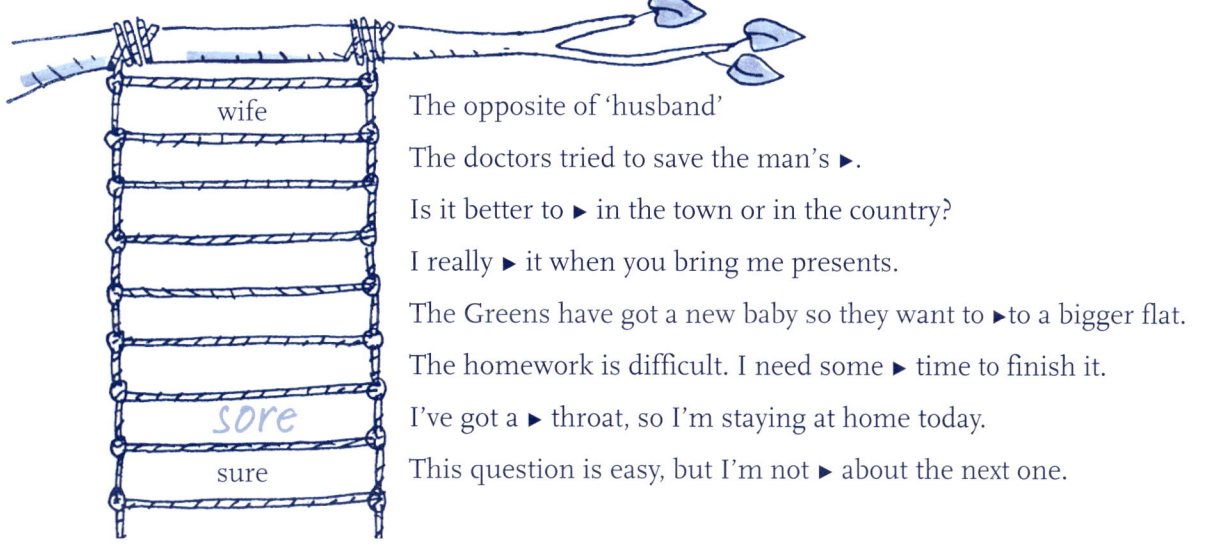

wife   The opposite of 'husband'

        The doctors tried to save the man's ▶.

        Is it better to ▶ in the town or in the country?

        I really ▶ it when you bring me presents.

        The Greens have got a new baby so they want to ▶ to a bigger flat.

        The homework is difficult. I need some ▶ time to finish it.

sore   I've got a ▶ throat, so I'm staying at home today.

sure   This question is easy, but I'm not ▶ about the next one.

Unit 5

New words ▸ *pp. 74 – 75*

Ich bin dran. Gib mir bitte die **Würfel**.	It's my turn. Give me the _____ please.
Wer ist an der Reihe?	_____ ?
Wessen Buch ist dies?	_____ book is this?
Ich kann **ein Feld vorgehen**.	I can _____ .
Nein, du musst **ein Feld zurück gehen**.	No, you have to _____ .
Jetzt muss ich **einmal aussetzen**.	Now I have to _____ .
Brunel war ein berühmter **Ingenieur**.	Brunel was a famous _____ .
Er hat diesen Bahnhof **gebaut**.	He _____ this station.
Die Stadt will eine neue Brücke **bauen**.	The city wants to _____ a new bridge.
Diese **Kneipe** ist über 300 Jahre alt.	This _____ is over 300 years old.
Warum ist der Laden heute **geschlossen**?	Why is the shop _____ today?
Wir kaufen unser Obst auf dem **Markt**.	We buy our fruit at the _____ .
Obst ist sehr **gesund**.	Fruit is very _____ .
Haben wir Zeit für einen **Imbiss**?	Do we have time for a _____ ?
In jenen Tagen gab es viele **Sklaven**.	In those days there were many _____ .
Papa mag **britische** Musik aus den Sechzigern.	Dad likes _____ music from the 60s.
Unsere neuen Nachbarn sind **Briten**.	Our new neighbours are _____ .
Sind sie **reich** oder arm?	Are they _____ or poor?
Sie haben viel Geld und auch **Grund und Boden**.	They've got lots of money and _____ too.
Welches **Land** würdest du gerne besuchen?	Which _____ would you like to visit?
Auf diesem Feld **bauen** sie Kartoffeln **an**.	They _____ potatoes in this field.
Brauchst du **Zucker** für deinen Tee?	Do you need _____ for your tea?
Sklaven haben in den **Tabak**feldern gearbeitet.	Slaves worked in the _____ fields.
Wann **kommt** der Flug **an**?	When does the flight _____ ?

1 A German-English crossword

Across

2 Markt (6)
4 Ehefrau (4)
6 ankommen (6)
7 anbauen (4)
9 berühmt (6)
11 Zucker (5)
12 Land (4)
14 reich (4)
16 er (2)
17 können (3)
19 Ingenieur (8)
21 zu (2)

Down

1 mir, mich (2)
2 meiner, meine meins (4)
3 läuten (3)
5 Feuerwehr-mann (7)
8 schwach (4)
9 fallen (4)
10 stark (10)
13 Würfel (4)
15 hoffen (4)
16 verletzt (4)
18 und (3)
20 kein/keine (2)

2 Spot the mistakes

In jedem Satz sind zwei Fehler. Finde und korrigiere sie.

1 You can get <u>idees</u> for your trip at the turist information.   *ideas* _____

2 Do you no what we can do hear in Bristol?   _____ _____

3 You can learn about sience at this exiting museum.   _____ _____

4 Or learn about slavs on the tobbaco farms in the Caribbean.   _____ _____

5 Or spend an our on the ice if you have enaugh time.   _____ _____

3 Word snail

Trage die englischen past participles der angegebenen Wörter in die Schnecke ein. Die Anfangsbuchstaben in der Schnecke helfen dir.

The secret words are:

New words ▸ *pp. 76 – 77*

Dies ist eine **Broschüre** über Bristol.   This is a _____ about Bristol.

Ich kenne einige **Einzelheiten** über die Stadt.   I know some _____ about the city.

Wir lesen immer die **örtliche** Zeitung.   We always read the _____ newspaper.

Hast du die **Statue** von Brunel gesehen?   Have you seen the _____ of Brunel?

Bitte **schreibt** diese Übung von der Tafel **ab**. Please _____ this exercise from the board.

Kann ich eine **Kopie** von deinem Buch machen?   Can I make a _____ of your book?

Oma **ist** 1948 **geboren**.   Grandma _____ in 1948.

Nach der Schule **wurde** sie Verkäuferin.   She _____ a shop assistant after school.

Hast du Angst vor **Tunnels**?   Are you afraid of _____ ?

Ja. Und ich habe **auch** Angst vor Pferden.   Yes. And I'm _____ afraid of horses.

Jedes Jahr **sterben** viele Menschen in Unfällen.   Many people _____ in accidents every year.

Unsere Eltern können **stolz auf** uns sein.   Our parents can be _____ us.

Bitte **markiere** die wichtigen Informationen.   Please _____ the important information.

4 Definitions

Vervollständige die Definitionen mit Wörtern aus dem Zettel.
Trage die richtigen Wörter von der Tafel in die rechte Spalte ein.

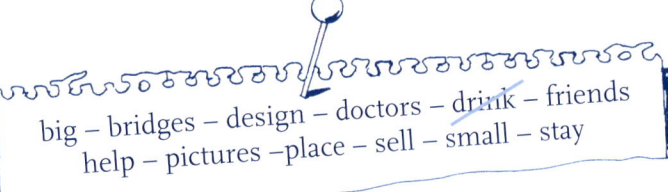

big – bridges – design – doctors – drink – friends
help – pictures –place – sell – small – stay

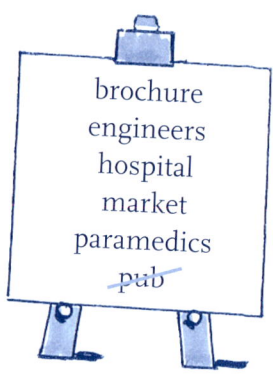

brochure
engineers
hospital
market
paramedics
pub

1 In this place people *drink* and talk to their _____ .   *pub*_____

2 They _____ you when you're ill, but they aren't _____ .   _____

3 a _____ building where you _____ when you're ill.   _____

4 a _____ book with information and _____   _____

5 People buy and_____ things at this _____ .   _____

6 They _____ and build _____ , etc.   _____

New words ▸ p. 78

Diese Pizza ist **köstlich**.	This pizza is _____ .
Ich kann es nicht machen – es ist **unmöglich**.	I can't do it – it's _____ .
Ist es **möglich**, mit dem Bus dorthin zu fahren?	Is it _____ to go there by bus?
Du **machst Witze, nicht wahr**?	You'_____ ?
Tim spielt **ziemlich** gut, aber Jo spielt besser.	Tim plays _____ well, but Jo plays better.
Magst du diese **Sorte**?	Do you like this _____ ?
Nein, ich mag keine **Erdbeeren**.	No, I don't like _____ .
Unsere **Kunden** mögen unseren Laden sehr.	Our _____ love our shop.
Der **Kellner** bringt uns gerade die Suppe.	The _____ is bringing us the soup now.
Kannst du die **Kellnerin** um Wasser bitten?	Can you ask the _____ for water?
Das **mittelgroße** Hemd passt sehr gut.	The _____ shirt fits very well.
Passt das **große** Hemd auch?	Does the _____ shirt fit too?
Brunel war ein **großer** Ingenieur.	Brunel was a _____ engineer.

5 Word search

Finde im Rätsel die gezeichneten Dinge und markiere sie. (   )

1

2

3

4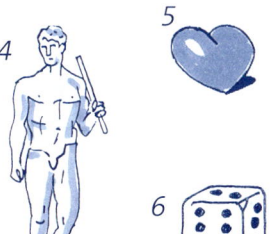

5

6

7

8

9

T	H	E	R	M	O	M	E	T	E	R	M
S	U	I	T	C	A	S	E	M	F	H	O
T	U	R	A	I	L	W	A	Y	A	Y	U
U	S	T	A	T	U	E	J	E	C	R	N
N	Y	Q	N	X	K	I	Z	L	T	C	T
N	N	U	G	E	T	I	C	E	O	C	A
E	O	F	E	A	N	F	Q	F	R	S	I
L	O	O	L	T	D	O	R	B	Y	H	N
H	E	A	R	T	M	R	I	C	B	E	S
P	C	A	S	T	L	E	V	Z	C	E	Y
P	Y	J	A	M	A	S	E	I	O	P	O
V	I	D	I	C	E	T	R	J	W	K	R

New words ▸ *pp. 79 – 84*

Ich habe den **Anfang** des Filmes verpasst.	I missed the _____ of the film.
Wann hat das Schiff den **Hafen** verlassen?	When did the ship leave the _____ ?
Hast du die **Matrosen** gesehen?	Did you see the _____ ?
Wie kann ich den Aufsatz besser **strukturieren**?	How can I _____ the essay better?
Ich brauche **Informationen** über Brunel.	I need _____ about Brunel.
Das war eine interessante **Diskussion**.	That was an interesting _____ .
Du hast Recht. Ich **stimme** dir **zu**.	You're right. I _____ you.
Ein **Tornado** kann sehr gefährlich sein.	A _____ can be very dangerous.

6 Odd word out

Unterstreiche das Wort, das nicht passt.

1 German – British – Bristol – French

2 build – see – smell – hear

3 grandchild – cousin – sister – family

4 kiwi – strawberry – dice – cherry

5 engineer – statue – teacher – fireman

6 terrible – famous – horrible – awful

7 tunnel – forest – road – bridge

8 play – practise – proud – prepare

9 tornado – weather – wind – storm

10 fine – healthy – ill – well

7 Word families

Vervollständige die Tabelle.

verb	noun
build	building
listen	
	drink
describe	
	collector
	invitation
copy	

8 Opposites

Trage die Gegenteile der fett gedruckten Wörter in die Lücken ein.

1 a **strong** / _____ man

2 Is the shop still **open** / _____ ?

3 He came from a very **poor** / _____ family.

4 When does your flight **leave** / _____ ?

5 the **end** / _____ of the film

6 a good **wife** / _____

7 She looks **healthy** / _____ .

8 Is this really **possible** / _____ ?

9 Numbers and letters

Zu jeder Zahl gehört ein Buchstabe. Finde die Lösungswörter und dann den „geheimen Satz".

1 Did the __ __ __ __ __ __ __ arrive at the fire on time?
$\quad$ 14 6 3 1 11 1 5

2 We have to write an essay for our history __ E __ __ __ __ R .
$\quad$ 4 1 8 2 12 1 3

3 The __ __ __ __ __ __ brought Jack some tea and cake.
$\quad$ 15 8 6 4 1 3

4 Brunel? He was a famous British __ __ __ __ __ __ __ __ .
$\quad$ 1 5 9 6 5 1 1 3

5 Sophie's aunt and uncle work at a hospital – they're both __ __ __ __ __ __ __ .
$\quad$ 17 10 2 4 10 3 16

6 She's a __ __ __ __ __ __ in a famous band.
$\quad$ 16 6 5 9 1 3

7 A __ __ __ __ __ __ __ __ __ __ stopped me because my bike had no lamp.
$\quad$ 7 10 13 6 2 1 15 10 11 8 5

8 Mike and Jane are __ __ __ __ __ __ __ __ __ __ __ __ __ in a pet shop.
$\quad$ 16 12 10 7 $\quad$ 8 16 16 6 16 4 8 5 4 16

The secret sentence is

__ __ __ __ , __ __ __ __ __ __ __ __ , __ __ __ __ __ __ __ __ B __ __ __ __ __ __ !
15 12 1 5 $\quad$ 6 11 $\quad$ 10 13 17 1 3 $\quad$ 6 15 8 5 4 $\quad$ 4 10 $\quad$ 18 1 $\quad$ 8 $\quad$ 16 4 8 3

Hey! Bei Berufen nimmt man dasselbe Wort für Frauen und Männer!

Richtig Ken ... dasselbe Wort. Mit wenigen Ausnahmen wie: policeman/policewoman waiter/waitress, ...

10 Word friends

Die Wörter in zwei Käsestücken passen zum Verb im Schild. Finde sie.

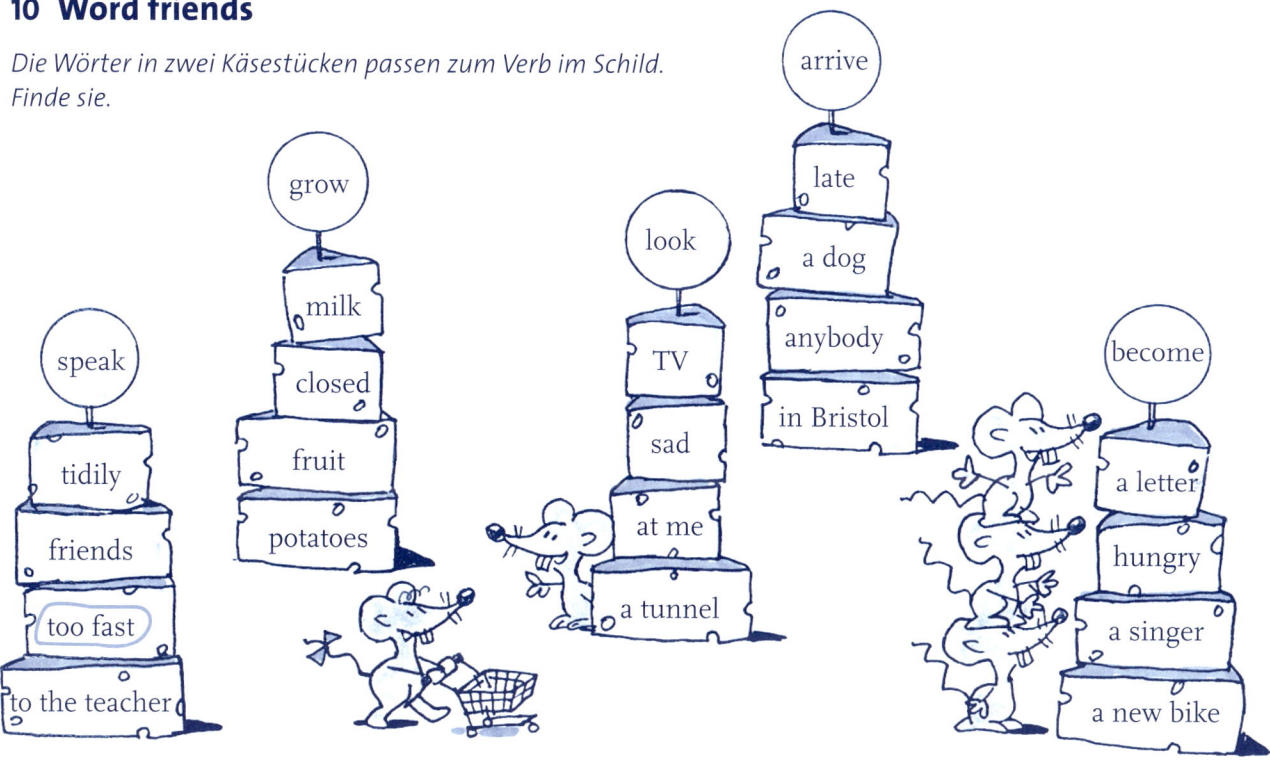

arrive: late, a dog, anybody, in Bristol

look: TV, sad, at me, a tunnel

grow: milk, closed, fruit, potatoes

speak: tidily, friends, too fast, to the teacher

become: a letter, hungry, a singer, a new bike

New words ▸ *pp. 86 – 88*

Wird die Polizei die Bankräuber **fangen**?	Will the police _____ the bank robbers?
Der **Dieb** versucht, das Auto zu stehlen.	The _____ is trying to steal the car.
Das wird ein **Fall** für die Polizei sein.	That will be a _____ for the police.
Plötzlich **verschwand** der Mann.	Suddenly the man _____ .
Jemand hat versucht, mein Handy zu **stehlen**.	Somebody tried to _____ my mobile.
Gestern **hat** jemand mein Geld **gestohlen**.	Yesterday somebody _____ my money.
Wer war da? **Wen** hast du gesehen?	Who was there? _____ did you see?
Verstehst du, was ich **meine**?	Do you understand what I _____ ?
Jane hat das Geld gestohlen. Ich habe **Beweise**.	Jane stole the money. I've got _____ .
Kim! Dein Zimmer sieht furchtbar aus! – **Na und**?	Kim! Your room looks terrible! – _____ ?
Hast du viel Geld in deiner **Geldbörse**?	Have you got much money in your _____ ?
Können wir uns **in der Pause** draußen treffen?	Can we meet outside _____ ?
Wo hast du deine **Schlüssel** verloren?	Where did you lose your _____ ?
Schöner **Ring**! Hast du viel Schmuck?	Nice _____ ! Do you have much jewellery?
Hör doch, etwas **piepst**.	Listen, something is _____ .
Ich kann keinen **Piepton** hören.	I can't hear a _____ .
Komm schnell, wenn ich **pfeife**.	Come quickly when I _____ .
Dann ging sie langsam **auf** mich **zu**.	Then she walked slowly _____ me.
Such deine Tasche! Wir haben es eilig!	_____ your bag! We're in a hurry!
Warte mal. Ist das unsere Straße?	_____ . Is this our road?
Lasst uns **hier entlang** gehen.	Let's go _____ .
Nein. Du gehst **in die falsche Richtung**.	No. You're going _____ .
Wir können den **Hausmeister** fragen.	We can ask the _____ .
Kannst du auf meine Tasche **aufpassen**?	Can you _____ my bag?
Hat die **Putzfrau** die Fenster sauber gemacht?	Has the _____ cleaned the windows?
Ich will nur einen Apfel. Nimm bitte den **Rest**.	I only want one apple. Please take the _____ .
Weiß **jemand**, wie spät es ist?	Does _____ know what the time is?

11 What are the words?

Welche Wörter passen in die Lücken.

1 There's <u>something</u> about Bristol on TV tonight.

2 Sophie didn't go _____ last Sunday. She was at home all day.

3 Look! _____ is waving at you. Is it Jack?

4 Where? I can't see _____ Oh yes, you're right. It is Jack.

5 I'm hungry but I haven't got _____ to eat.

6 Well, maybe we can have a snack _____ .

somebody   something   somewhere
anybody   anything   anywhere

12 Word groups

Trage die Wörter aus der Wiese in die richtige Blume ein.

food — popcorn

places in a town — shop

family

rooms — living room

aunt   bar   bathroom   bedroom   café   cinema   cousin   daughter   department store
dining-room   grandson   hall   hamburger   husband   kitchen   living-room   meat   orange
popcorn   pizza   pub   salad   shop   strawberry   toilet   wife

Unit 6

New words ▶ p. 92

Dies ist eine alte **römische** Straße.

This is an old _____ road.

Und dies ist ein römisches **Bad**.

And this is a Roman _____ .

Sezten wir uns an den **runden** Tisch.

Let's sit down at the _____ table.

Es ist schön, mit Freunden zu **plaudern**.

It's nice to _____ with friends.

Lass uns später **in die Sauna gehen**.

Let's _____ later.

Wir können uns dort **ausruhen**.

We can _____ there.

Es gibt eine große **Mauer** um den Garten.

There's a big _____ round the garden.

Wir bauten das Haus aus Holz und **Stein**.

We built the house with wood and _____ .

1 Lost words

Ergänze die Sätze mit den angesprühten Wörtern.

1 Bath is about 12 miles southeast __*of*__ Bristol.

2 The city is famous _____ its Roman buildings.

3 The Romans came _____ Britain in the year 43.

4 They stayed there _____ about 450.

5 _____ 43 and 25 they built lots of towns.

6 And they built roads, so people could travel faster _____ town to town.

7 The most important town _____ Roman Britain was London.

8 The Roman name _____ London was Londinium

for   between   from
of   to   in
till
for

2 Odd word out

Ein Wort passt nicht. Finde und unterstreiche es.

1 door – window – park – wall

2 beautiful – round – nice – pretty

3 famous – large – medium – small

4 house – church – building – school

5 Roman – German – London – British

6 cheese – bread – meat – stone

7 relax – armchair – bed – sofa

8 speak – chat – write – talk

New words ▸ p. 94

Es ist nur eine kurze **Fahrradfahrt**.

It's only a short _____ .

Es gibt schöne **Pfade** durch den Wald.

There are nice _____ through the forest.

Wie geht es Ihnen Frau Carter-Brown?

_____ Mrs Carter-Brown?

Lasst uns **mit dem Fahrrad** nach Hause **fahren**.

Let's _____ home.

Wieviele **Planeten** gibt es?

How many _____ are there?

Schau dir all die **Sterne** am Himmel an.

Look at all the _____ in the sky.

3 The fourth word

Welches Wort fehlt hier?

1 magazine – read / clothes – _____

2 earrings – ears / shoes – _____

3 cap – head / trousers – _____

4 hand – fingers / foot – _____

5 eyes – see / nose – _____

6 head – headache / ear – _____

7 rainy – rain / foggy – _____

8 hot – cold / warm – _____

9 day – sun / night – _____

10 fireman – firewoman / waiter – _____

11 ship – sailor / car – _____

12 car – garage / ship – _____

13 fast – slow / happy – _____

14 noisy – quiet / strong – _____

4 Word web

_Übersetze die Wörter und trage
sie in das Spinnennetz ein.
Alle englischen Wörter haben
den gleichen Endbuchstaben._

1 jeder, jede, jedes
2 neblig
3 schmutzig
4 leer
5 lustig
6 wütend, böse
7 früh
8 glücklich
9 heute
10 Tagebuch
11 Feind
12 bereit, fertig

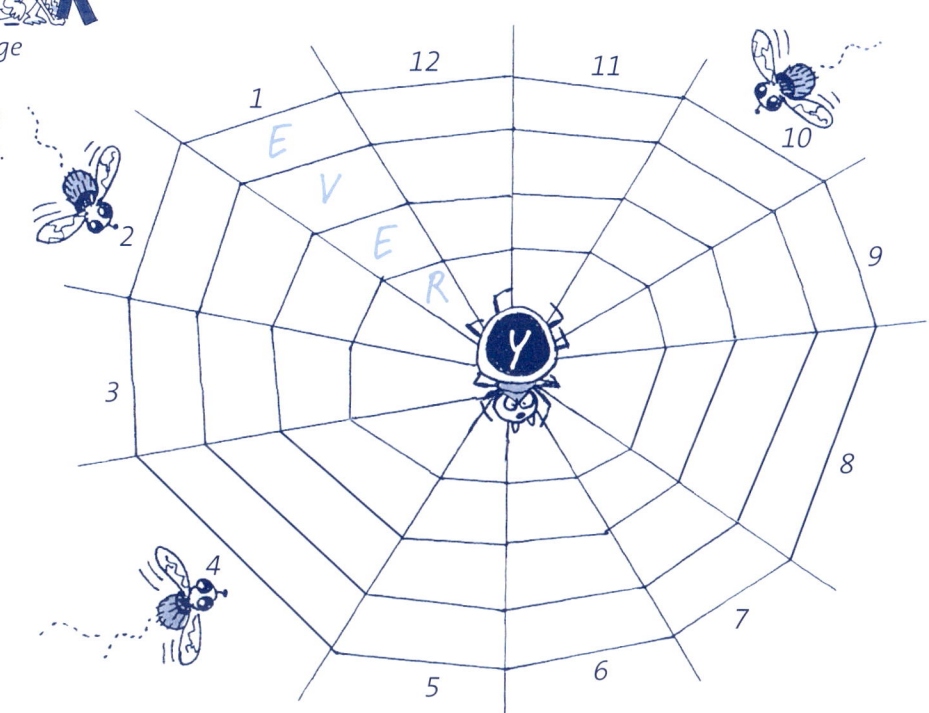

New words ▶ p. 95

Hast du einen **Stadtplan** von Berlin?	Have you got a _____ of Berlin?
Kannst du mir **den Weg** dorthin **beschreiben**?	Can you _____ me _____ there?
Oder ich kann Jo **nach dem Weg fragen**.	Or I can _____ Jo _____ .
Biege rechts **ab** und geh **geradeaus weiter**.	_____ right and go _____ .
Geh am **Postamt vorbei**.	Go _____ the _____ .
Dann müsst ihr die Brücke **überqueren**.	Then you have to _____ the bridge.
Die Bank ist an der **Ecke**	The bank is on the _____
... neben dem **Polizeirevier**.	... next to the _____ .
Das Essen im diesem **Restaurant** ist gut.	The food in this _____ is good.
Gibt es eine **Apotheke** in dieser Straße?	Is there a _____ in this street?

5 Words with different meanings

Finde in der Liste die passenden Wörter zu den Paaren 1–10.
Trage sie ein und unterstreiche die deutschen Entsprechungen.

Ihr wisst schon: Manche Wörter haben mehr als eine Bedeutung!

1
a) ein Stern am Himmel
b) der Star der Show
star

4
a) die Fenster putzen
b) saubere Fenster

6
a) Öffne bitte das Fenster!
b) Ist der Laden geöffnet?

7
a) Der Film ist vorbei.
b) über die Brücke

2
a) bevor ich gehe
b) Er war schon mal hier.

8
a) Beweg dich nicht!
b) Wir wollen bald umziehen.

9
a ein rundes Zimmer
b) um die Burg herum

3
a) Ein Punkt für unser Team!
b) auf jemanden zeigen

5
a) Lass uns zu Fuß gehen!
b) einen Spaziergang machen

10
a) am Postamt vorbei
b) Vergangenheit und Zukunft

walk
past
before
round
move
open
over
point
clean
star

6 Hour glasses

Übersetze die Wörter und trage sie in die passende Sanduhr ein.

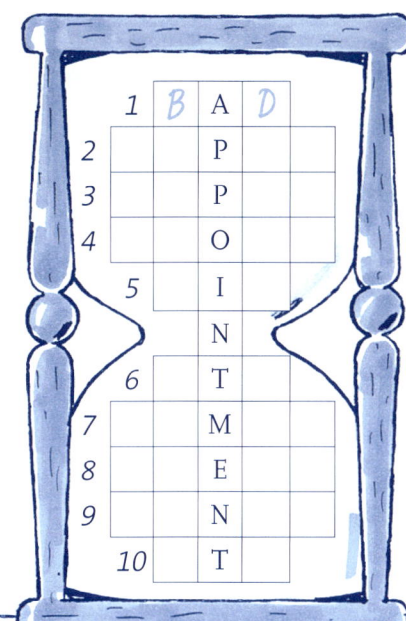

1 Ei – schlimm

2 leer – groß

3 Zeitung – Herz

4 überqueren – sonnig

5 groß – hinzufügen

6 Landkarte – sein(e)/ihr(e)

7 römisch – Bäder

8 andere(r, s) – träumen

9 Monat – piepsen

10 Kunst – aß

Die senkrechten Wörter in den Sanduhren heißen: links _____

rechts _____

7 Word search

Finde im Gitter die Wörter,
die in den Ausdrücken fehlen.

1 *drink* _____ milk

2 _____ a thief

3 _____ a text

4 _____ a house

5 _____ the road

6 _____ right

7 _____ to school

8 _____ a song

9 _____ a sauna

10 _____ a skirt

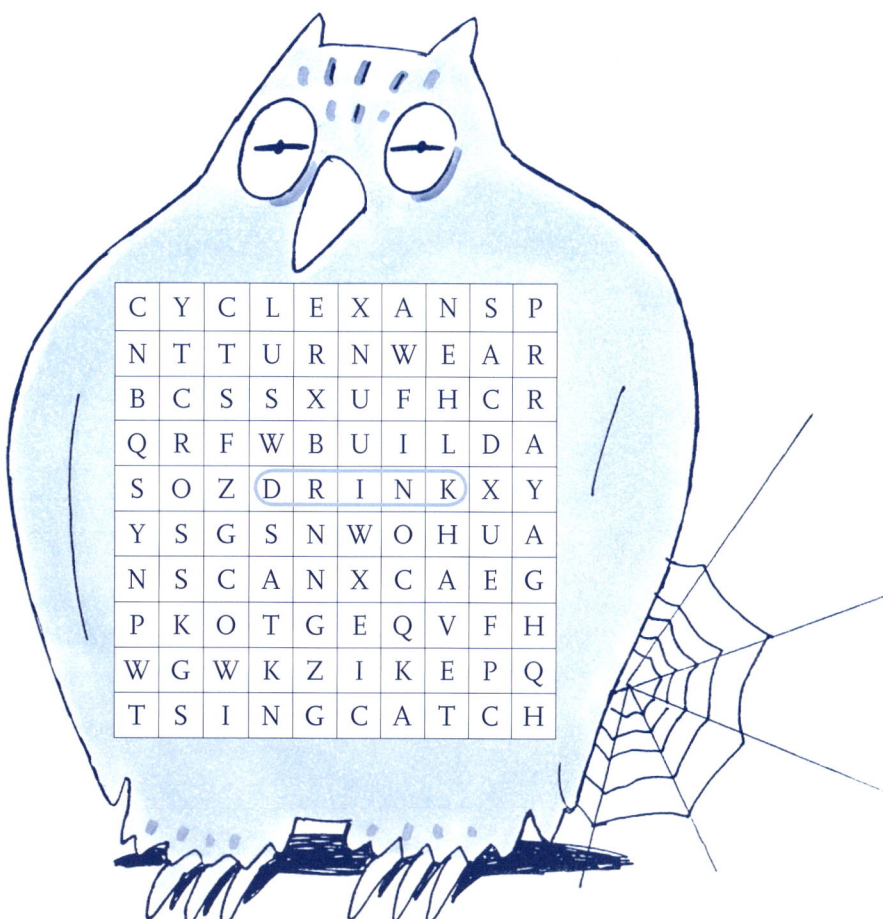

C	Y	C	L	E	X	A	N	S	P
N	T	T	U	R	N	W	E	A	R
B	C	S	S	X	U	F	H	C	R
Q	R	F	W	B	U	I	L	D	A
S	O	Z	D	R	I	N	K	X	Y
Y	S	G	S	N	W	O	H	U	A
N	S	C	A	N	X	C	A	E	G
P	K	O	T	G	E	Q	V	F	H
W	G	W	K	Z	I	K	E	P	Q
T	S	I	N	G	C	A	T	C	H

New words ▸ *pp. 96 - 102*

Ich sehe nur neun Kinder. Wer **fehlt**?	I only see nine kids. Who _____ ?
Wir **brauchen nicht** auf Tim zu warten.	We _____ wait for Tim.
Wir **dürfen** den Raum **nicht** verlassen.	We _____ leave the room.
Hi, **hier spricht** Jo. Ist Jack zu Hause?	Hi, _____ Jo. Is Jack at home?
Sie gingen die Straße **entlang**.	They walked _____ the road.
Lasst uns unserem Lehrer **einen Streich spielen**!	Let's _____ on our teacher!
Genieß den Tag auf der Schlittschuhbahn!	_____ the day at the _____ !
Bitte **verbessert** alle Fehler.	Please _____ all the mistakes.

8 What are the words?

Welche Wörter passen in die Lücken?

1 I __*must*__ get a present for Ananda. It's her birthday tomorrow.

2 And I _____ forget to buy a birthday card for her.

3 The party starts at four o'clock. I _____ be late.

4 But I don't know where she lives. I _____ find out her address.?

5 Oh. She lives very near us! So I _____ get a bus.

> must   must   mustn't
> mustn't   needn't.

9 Definitions

Vervollständige die Definitionen mit Wörtern aus den Mauersteinen.
Trage die richtigen Wörter aus Kens Zeitung in die rechte Spalte ein.

> department store
> map
> stars
> correct
> teenager
> post office

	between	buy	change	city	mistakes	see	
	send	shop	sky	way	stamps	way	young	

1 You often __see__ them in the _____ at night.   __stars__

2 A plan: it helps you find the _____ in a town or _____ . _____

3 A very big _____ : you can _____ lots of different things there. _____

4 a place where you can buy _____ or _____ parcels   _____

5 a _____ person, _____ 13 and 19 years old   _____

6 look for _____ and _____ them to make them right   _____

10 Word snake

*In der Schlange sind zehn Infinitive versteckt.
Finde sie und ergänze die Tabelle.*

Denkt dran:
Bei unregelmäßigen
Verben immer alle
drei Teile lernen!

fly	flew	
feel		felt

Snake letters: texreadnyputbcsit ... wszd iε dirrutreddihlhkwa ... kepstuegnisswqpwor ... xinzhcaetloiwesoohcpr ... himflymopfeelywrbring

11 Word ladder

*Gehe von unten nach oben, indem du bei jeder
Sprosse einen Buchstaben veränderst.*

well

feed

need

I don't feel ★ – I think I have temperature.

When ★ you be here tomorrow?

We climbed ★ we got to the top of the mountain.

Like a mountain, but smaller.

When you go through the front door you're in the ★.

It's round and you can play games with it.

saw – see / fell – ★

Poor Jo. He ★ and hurt his leg yesterday.

go – went – gone / feel – felt – ★

fingers – hands / toes – ★

The cats are hungry again. Can you ★ them, please.

You'll ★ a bike if you want to cycle to school.

New words ▶ pp. 103 – 105

Das Sommer**trimester** fängt in April an.

The summer _____ starts in April.

Kannst du ein Känguru **pantomimisch darstellen**?

Can you _____ a kangaroo?

Ich **mag** Judo **lieber** als Hockey.

I _____ judo _____ than hockey.

Glücklicherweise war niemand verletzt.

_____ nobody was hurt.

Wer ist dein Lieblings**schauspieler**?

Who's your favourite _____ ?

Plötzlich **fiel** Jo von seinem Fahrrad **herunter**.

Suddenly Jo _____ his bike.

Nein! **Anders herum** bitte!

No. The _____ please!

Ich hörte die **Bewegung** des Wassers.

I heard the _____ of the water.

Viel Spaß im **Freizeitpark**!

Have fun at the _____ !

Er **gähnte** und ging ins Bett.

He _____ and went to bed.

Hat die Show dem **Publikum** gefallen?

Did the _____ like the show?

Hurra! Ferien!

_____ ! Holidays!

Wie viel muss ich da**für bezahlen**?

How much do I have to _____ this?

Sind **Tomaten** und **Kopfsalat** gesund?

Are _____ and _____ healthy?

Brunel lebte im 19. **Jahrhundert**.

Brunel lived in the 19th _____ .

Ich **frage mich**, warum er **jubelt**.

I _____ why he's _____ .

Es gab Spaß und **Gelächter** auf der Party.

There was fun and _____ at the party.

Ich habe keine **Sorgen**, wenn ich in Urlaub bin.

I have no _____ when I'm on holiday.

Im Sommer wird es sehr früh **hell**.

In summer it gets _____ very early.

Ich weiß nicht, **ob** die Geschichte **wahr** ist.

I don't know _____ the story is _____ .

12 Word pairs

Welche Wörter passen zusammen?

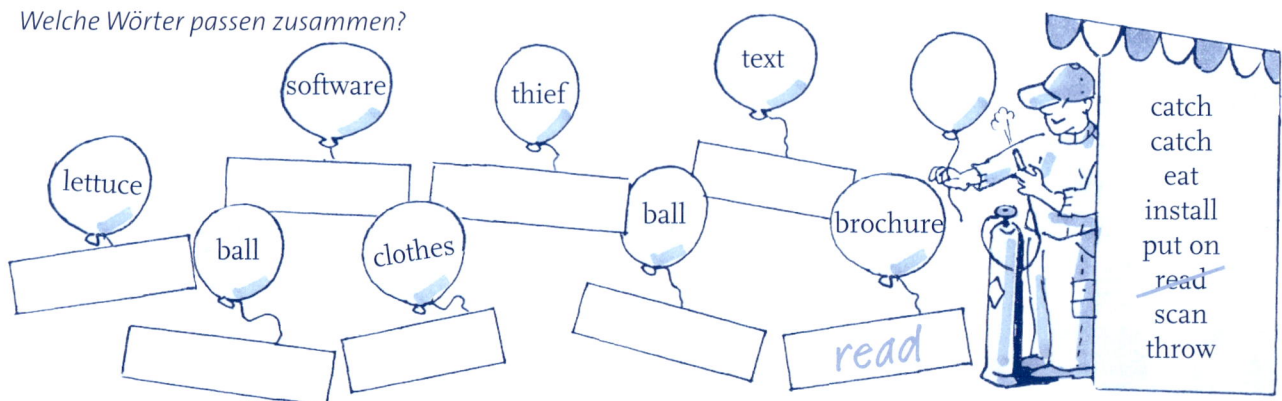

software · thief · text · lettuce · ball · clothes · ball · brochure · read

catch
catch
eat
install
put on
read
scan
throw

13 Pronunciation

Vervollständige die Listen mit Wörtern aus dem Zettel.
In jeder Liste müssen sich die Wörter reimen.

Markiere für jede Liste das passende Lautschriftsymbol.

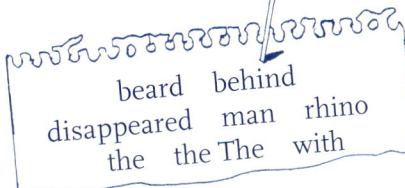

bought – caught – cheer – deer
flight – grew – here – quite
sport – threw – true – white

cheer ɔː	bright ɔː	_____ ɔː	_____ ɔː
dear (ɪə)	_____ ɪə	_____ ɪə	brought ɪə
_____ aɪ	_____ aɪ	through aɪ	_____ aɪ
_____ uː	_____ uː	_____ uː	_____ uː

Ordne die Lautschrift dem Wort zu.

1 'rɪəli   disappear
2 bɪəd   really
3 ˌdɪsə'pɪə   beard

4 'saɪkl   behind
5 bɪ'haɪnd   cycle
6 ˌaɪ 'tiː   IT

7 muːv   few
8 'fjuː   proof
9 pruːf   move

10 ɪn'stɔːl   thought
11 θɔːt   important
12 ɪm'pɔːtnt   install

Ordne die englischen Wörter der Lautschrift zu,
um den geheimen Satz zu finden.

beard   behind
disappeared   man   rhino
the   the   The   with

_____

ðə   mæn   wɪð   ðə   bɪəd   ˌdɪsə'pɪəd

_____

bɪ'haɪnd   ðə   'raɪnəʊ

14 Picture puzzle

Finde 7 weitere Dinge.

bath   _____

_____   _____

_____

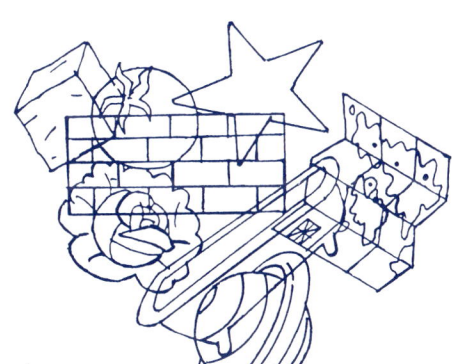

15 Crossword

Across

1 Please ★ the mistakes in your essay. (7)
2 a 'house' or 'hotel' behind a car (7)
6 see – ★ – seen (3)
9 lose – lost – ★ (4)
12 ★ 5 and 4 and you get 9. (3)
13 opposite of 'before' (5)
14 American English – elevator / British English ★ (4)
16 ★ – left – left (5)
18 Can you ★ the software please? (7)
20 throw – ★ – thrown (5)
21 We ★ tomatoes in our garden. (4)
23 speak – ★ – spoken (5)
24 opposite of 'poor' (4)
26 another word for 'speak' (4)
27 a very strong wind (7)
30 You throw this away because you don't want it. (7)
32 opposite of 'background' (10)
35 another word for 'little' (5)
38 What was the thief like? Can you ★ him please? (8)
40 opposite of 'everybody' (6)
42 The languages of Wales are English and ★. (5)
43 bring – ★ – brought (7)

Down

1 opposite of 'warm' (4)
2 Germany and France are ★. (9)
3 The Elbe is a ★ in Germany. (5)
4 My name is Alex – I'm ★ the top of the list. (2)
5 I've ★ the table, so we can have lunch now. (4)
7 opposite of 'strong' (4)
8 You wear this on your head, but not for baseball. (3)
10 a famous person or something in the sky (4)
11 This person cleans houses, flats or other buildings. (7)
15 feel – ★ – felt (4)
16 German – Gelächter / English – ★ (8)
17 We ★ from London to New York in seven hours. (4)
19 stand – stood – ★ (5)
22 a word for shirt, jeans, jacket (7)
25 man – men / hero – ★ (6)
28 another word for 'terrible' (5)
29 go – ★ – gone (4)
31 he – she – ★ (2)
33 If you add blue to yellow, you get ★. (5)
34 If you ★ in the cupboard, nobody will find you. (4)
36 eat – ★ – eaten (3)
37 like something very much (4)
39 Jo can't go to school today because he's ★. (3)
41 opposite of 'small' (3)

Lösungen

Welcome back

1 Numbers and letters
weather, cold, rainy, sun, clouds, mountains, snow, snow, storms, good, place, warm, sunny, weather. The secret sentence: *Wind and rain, clouds and snow – hurry up! It's time to go.*

2 The fourth word
1 cold, 2 warm, 3 rain, 4 those, 5 winter, 6 cloudy, 7 throw, 8 take, 9 rode, 10 country

3 Odd word out
1 sun, 2 library, 3 glasses, 4 stage, 5 caravan, 6 she

4 Lost words
1 for, 2 on, 3 of, 4 to, 5 in, 6 by, 7 at, 8 into

5 Word snake
1 island, 2 beach, 3 caravan, 4 glue, 5 theatre, 6 library, 7 view, 8 sky, 9 corner, 10 cloud, 11 country, 12 price

6 Word pairs
book: read, **clothes:** wear, **door:** knock, **photos:** take, **bed:** sleep, **mistake:** make, **plane:** fly

7 Spot the mistakes
1 eated: ate, Anandas: Ananda's
2 flied: flew, yier: year
3 rided: rode, baik: bike
4 she: her, comed: came
5 taked: took, cais: case
6 meeted: met, childs: children

8 Bits and pieces
1 country – Land
2 theatre – Theater
3 island – Insel
4 anyway – trotzdem
5 weather – Wetter
6 postcard – Postkarte
7 caravan – Wohnwagen
8 travel – reisen
9 something – etwas
10 moutain – Berg

9 What's the word: much or many?
a) 1 ~~much~~/many 2 much/~~many~~, 3 much/~~many~~, 4 ~~much~~/many 5 ~~much~~/many
b) 1 music, 2 exercises, 3 English grammar, 4 bread, 5 hobbies

10 Crossword
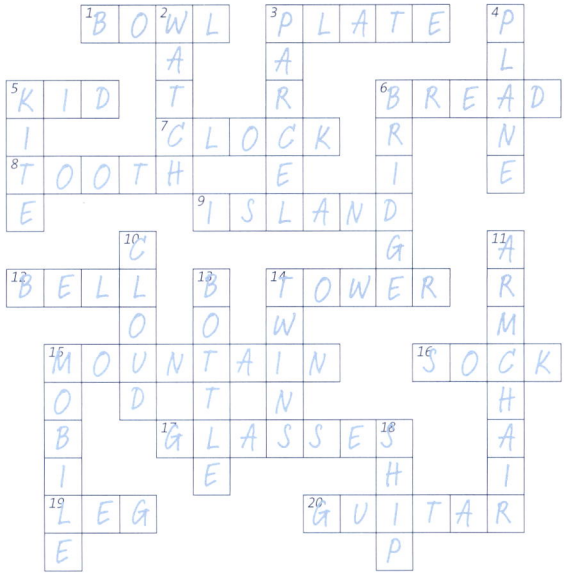

11 Word search

C	R	I	S	P	S	C	W	Q	B	I	S	C	U	I	T
H	D	T	O	O	T	H	S	A	U	S	A	G	E	Q	T
I	S	Q	P	T	O	E	F	S	O	V	G	G	R	W	I
C	Y	B	G	Q	H	E	Y	H	Q	I	S	R	M	B	M
K	S	A	U	N	T	S	A	I	U	P	T	A	I	O	E
E	O	F	I	S	H	E	D	R	J	A	U	N	C	O	T
N	C	G	X	J	P	B	A	T	C	R	D	D	E	T	A
V	K	R	M	L	O	O	U	F	L	R	E	P	M	S	B
J	S	A	O	E	T	A	G	H	A	O	N	A	B	R	L
U	D	N	U	G	A	R	H	A	S	T	T	R	X	A	E
N	R	D	T	M	T	D	T	N	S	D	U	E	S	B	W
C	B	C	H	N	O	M	E	D	R	R	A	N	H	B	M
L	R	H	E	M	Q	J	R	V	T	O	P	T	O	I	O
E	E	I	A	C	H	I	L	D	R	E	N	S	E	T	U
C	A	L	D	T	E	A	C	H	E	R	Q	F	S	T	S
H	K	D	H	D	R	E	S	S	S	N	A	K	E	E	E

Clothes:
top – Oberteil, boots – Stiefel, shirt – Hemd, shoes – Schuhe, socks – Socken, dress – Kleid
Family:
aunt – Tante, daughter – Tochter, grandparents – Großeltern, children – Kinder, grandchild – Enkel/in, uncle – Onkel

School:
teacher – Lehrer/in, student – Schüler/in,
board – Tafel, timetable – Stundenplan,
break – Pause, class – Klasse
Pets:
snake – Schlange, parrot – Papagei,
rabbit – Kaninchen, mouse – Maus,
mice – Mäuse, fish – Fisch
Food:
cheese – Käse, chicken – Huhn, biscuit – Keks,
crisps – Chips, potato – Kartoffel, sausage – Wurst
Parts of the body:
hand – Hand, tooth – Zahn, head – Kopf,
leg – Bein, toe – Zeh, mouth – Mund

Unit 1

1 Word families
1 rehearse/rehearsal
2 describe/description
3 drink/drink
4 invite/invitation
5 live/life
6 dance/dance

2 What are the words?
1 near the lake
2 on the left
3 behind the tree
4 at the bottom of the mountain
5 in the foreground
6 under water

3 Crossword

4 Scrambled words
1 church, 2 theatre, 3 shop, 4 School,
5 Tower, 6 bridge, 7 station, 8 library,
9 museum, 10 house
The secret word: *crocodiles*

5 The fourth word
1 foreground, 2 slow, 3 at the bottom,
4 knew, 5 behind, 6 toe, 7 her, 8 hutch,
9 description, 10 taught

6 Odd word out
1 dangerous, 2 bedroom, 3 cooker,
4 choir, 5 loud, 6 bike, 7 cards, 8 go

7 Word search

1 interesting/boring
2 great/terrible
3 good/bad
4 easy/difficult
5 quiet/loud
6 hot/cold
7 nice/rude
8 right/wrong
9 cool/warm
10 fast/slow

8 Word snail
describe, dangerous, background, lake,
between, slow, speak, clothes, cooker,
foggy, flight, rude
The secret words: *back to school*

9 Plurals
1 **Mann** – man – **men**
2 **Frau** – woman – **women**
3 Zahn – **tooth** – **teeth**
4 **Kind** – child – **children**
5 **Foto** – photo – **photos**
6 Kartoffel – **potato** – **potatoes**
7 **Quiz/Ratespiel** – quiz – **quizzes**
8 Kasten – **box** – **boxes**
9 **Leben** – life – **lives**
10 **Held/Heldin** – hero – **heroes**
11 **Maus** – **mouse** – mice
12 Fuß – **foot** – **feet**
13 **Land** – country – **countries**

14 Aufsatz – **essay** – **essays**
15 **Familie** – **family** – families
16 Hobby – **hobby** – **hobbies**

10 Picture puzzle

caravan, clock, elephant, parcel/present, pirate, plane, ship, stamp

11 Word ladder

home, **some**, **same**, **game**, **gave**, **give**, **live**, **like**, bike

12 Lost words

1 light ... on, *2* bottom of
3 calm down, *4* for ... walk
5 for miles, *6* by car
7 thing about, *8* angry with

13 Spot the mistakes

1 flait: flight, too: to
2 gos: goes, bai: by
3 sea: see, on: in
4 match: much, paunds: pounds
5 happi: happy, idee: idea
6 Finnish: Finish, bevor: before
7 engry: angry, misteaks: mistakes

14 Word groups

sports and hobbies:
collect stamps, go surfing, go swimming, make models, play the guitar, skate
theatre:
act, play, rehearse, scene, show, ticket
head:
ears, eyes, face, hair, mouth, nose, teeth
travel:
bike, boat, bus, car, plane, ship, train

15 Word web

1 after, *2* answer, *3* water, *4* colour,
5 guitar, *6* wear, *7* cooker, *8* never,
9 father, *10* hour, *11* letter, *12* number

Unit 2

1 Scrambled words: clothes

1 skirt, *2* sweatshirt, *3* trousers,
4 pullover, *5* jacket, *6* trainers
The secret word: *shorts*

2 Odd word out

1 wear, *2* beach, *3* ship, *4* make-up,
5 budgie, *6* sad

3 Word search

bathroom, bed, chair, clock, cooker, cupboard, dishwasher, door, fridge, kitchen, shelf, shower, stairs, toilet, wardrobe, window

D	C	S	C	P	T	C	H	A	I	R	B
O	D	H	R	F	S	T	A	I	R	S	E
O	I	O	B	K	I	T	C	H	E	N	D
R	S	W	A	R	D	R	O	B	E	J	W
O	H	E	Q				C	J	U	I
C	W	R	E				U	P	M	N
O	A	M	D				P	T	S	D
O	S	B	N				B	O	H	O
K	H	F	R	I	D	G	E	O	I	E	W
E	E	N	U	U	J	G	D	A	L	L	P
R	R	W	C	L	O	C	K	R	E	F	E
B	A	T	H	R	O	O	M	D	T	P	H

4 Word snake

1 heard/hear
2 understood/understand
3 bought/buy
4 won/win
5 thought/think
6 found/find
7 wore/wear
8 sold/sell
9 taught/teach
10 knew/know

5 Lost words

1 Hers, *2* yours, *3* mine, *4* theirs,
5 his, *6* ours

6 The fourth word

1 cinema, *2* lost, *3* spent, *4* ours,
5 legs, *6* shelves, *7* ride, *8* countries,
9 everybody, *10* stupid, *11* cage,
12 building, *13* hour, *14* mine

7 Words with different meanings

1 save: retten, sparen
2 meet: kennenlernen, treffen
3 know: wissen, kennen
4 right: richtige, rechten
5 show: Show, zeigen
6 free: freier, kostenlose
7 before: vor, bevor
8 present: Gegenwart, Geschenk
9 cool: cool, kühl
10 look: aussehen, schauen

8 What are the words?
1 the youngest, *2* hotter, *3* cheaper,
4 the best, *5* older, *6* the biggest

9 Bits and pieces
 1 letter – Brief
 2 survey – Umfrage/Untersuchung
 3 Mountain – Berg
 4 problem – Problem
 5 everybody – jeder/alle
 6 trousers – Hose
 7 cinema – Kino
 8 describe – beschreiben
 9 fuller – voller
10 person – Person
11 always – immer
12 amazing – erstaunlich/unglaublich

10 Word friends
a) **do**: an exercise, a project, sport, tricks
   have: a drink, an idea, a party, fun
   make: a film, a noise, a mistake, the bed
b) 1 make a noise
    2 have a drink
    3 do sport
    4 have an idea
    5 Have fun
    6 do a project

11 Opposites
1 black, *2* love, *3* worst *4* big, *5* cheap,
6 won, *7* found, *8* interesting/exciting,
9 after, *10* fast, *11* top, *12* background

12 Pronunciation
1 one, run, sun, won (ʌ)
2 fair, pair, prepare, there (eə)
3 design, fine, mine shine (aɪ)
4 flew, threw, through, who (uː)

1 country, *2* son, *3* bunk, *4* stairs,
5 scared, *6* careful, *7* describe, *8* eye,
9 island, *10* rude, *11* cool, *12* ruler
The secret sentence: *I'd like to be on an
island where the sun always shines.*

13 Word groups
food: cheese, chicken, chips, potatoes, sausages
clothes: boots, shirt, shoes, skirt, top
pets: dog, cat, guinea pig, mouse, parrot

Unit 3

1 Scrambled words: pets
1 guinea pig, *2* rabbit, *3* fish, *4* tortoise,
5 horse, *6* dog, *7* budgie, *8* hamster
The 'secret pet' is a parrot.

2 Word search: wild animals

H	I	W	W	W	V
E	S	R	F	O	X
D	Q	F	R	O	G
G	U	M	G	D	Y
E	I	O	L	P	E
H	R	L	B	E	E
O	R	E	U	C	M
G	E	J	B	K	R
R	L	O	E	E	P
S	D	E	E	R	D

fox – Fuchs
frog – Frosch
deer – Reh
hedgehog – Igel
squirrel – Eichhörnchen
mole – Maulwurf
woodpecker – Specht

3 Word snail
sang, made, hid, slept, let, put, lost,
wrote, gave, chose, brought, fed
The secret words are: *Smile please!*

4 Word ladder
most, **lost**, **lose**, **love**, **live five**, **fine**, find

5 Definitions
1 grey, trees – **squirrel**
2 shoes, sport – **trainers**
3 sky, shines – **moon**
4 building, watch – **films**
5 throw, bin – **rubbish**
6 word, ready – **prepare**

6 Odd word out
1 grey, *2* sleep, *3* holiday, *4* bigger,
5 person, *6* yard

7 Fourth word
1 dustbin, *2* moon, *3* garage, *4* won't be,
5 colour, *6* explanation

8 Numbers and letters
1 slowly, clearly, *2* angrily, *3* quickly,
4 happily, *5* carefully, *6* nervously,
7 loudly
The secret sentence: *Dad always drives slowly
and carefully on rainy days.*

9 Picture puzzle
camel, elephant, giraffe, hippo, kangaroo,
lion, zebra

10 Spot the mistakes

1 <u>serie</u>: series, <u>programes</u>: programmes
2 <u>Their</u>: There, <u>then</u>: than
3 <u>fokses</u>: foxes, <u>citys</u>: cities
4 <u>too</u>: two, <u>dastbin</u>: dustbin
5 <u>well</u>: good, <u>wants</u>: want

11 Word groups

Holiday <u>We went by</u> ... car, plane, ship, train
<u>We stayed in a</u> ... bed and breakfast, caravan, hotel
Clothes <u>Only for girls!</u> top, dress, skirt
<u>For boys and girls</u> hat, pullover, shirt, shoes, socks, trousers
Weather <u>It was</u> ... cold, cool, foggy, stormy, sunny, windy <u>Look at the</u> ... clouds, rain, snow

12 Crossword

	C	A	R	A	V	A	N			M			S	P	O	K	E	
H							I	L	L		M			N	
E		S	T	O	O	D		N		G	L	A	S	S	E	S
A				E	N	E	M	Y		L			W	
P	O	I	N	T	S			S	L	O	W	
F		D	R	A	N	K		H		N
L	O	V	E	W		L	A	I	D	N	O
D	O	U	S	F		N	O	B
N	G	R	C	O	U	N	T	R	I	E	S	T	O
D	U	S	T	B	I	N	A	F	R	A	I	N	Y
W	O	R	E	E	X	C	I	T	I	N	G	A
L	F	E	L	T	H	A	B	O	U	T
B	O	U	G	H	T
F	R	O	G	H	O	U	R
G	A	R	A	G	E	C	I	N	E	M	A
T	I	D	Y

Unit 4

1 What's the word: *in* or *on*?

1 in/in, 2 in/auf, 3 on/an, 4 on/im,
5 in/am, 6 on/am, 7 in/am, 8 on/im

2 Word families

Verb	Noun
visit	**visit**
explain	explanation
fly	flight
describe	**description**
answer	**answer**
glue	glue
paint	**painter**

1 explain, 2 visit, 3 fly, 4 painter,
5 description

3 Odd word out

1 picnic, 2 paint, 3 river, 4 Germany,
5 cook, 6 sights, 7 farm, 8 woodpecker,
9 yard, 10 noise, 11 dirty, 12 mountain

4 Word snake

1 be – was – been
2 make – made – made
3 eat – ate – eaten
4 take – took – taken
5 go – went – gone
6 see – saw – seen
7 do – did – done
8 have – had – had
9 come – came – come
10 find – found – found

5 Word friends

1 **do**: a good job, an exercise
2 **go**: by car, for a walk
3 **make**: breakfast, an appointment
4 **have**: a birthday party, a baby

6 The fourth word

1 clean, 2 interview, 3 paragraph, 4 noisy/loud,
5 smell, 6 taken, 7 sheep, 8 Welsh

7 Word mix

1 Let's go on holiday to Wales.
2 There are lots of old castles there.
3 You'll see mounains, hills and valleys.
4 The railway museum is an interesting place.
5 Many Welsh people speak Welsh.
6 But everybody speaks English too.
7 So we won't have problems with the language.

8 Hour glasses

1	A	G	O	
2	A	G	R	E	E
3	B	E	A	C	H
4	F	U	N	N	Y
5	A	D	D	
	M		
6	D	O	G	
7	W	A	T	C	H
8	O	T	H	E	R
9	B	R	E	A	K
10	A	R	E	

1	B	E	D	
2	F	O	X	E	S
3	E	M	P	T	Y
4	S	A	L	A	D
5	B	A	D	
	N		
6	W	A	S	
7	H	A	T	E	D
8	N	O	I	S	E
9	F	L	O	O	R
10	E	N	D	

Die senkrechten Wörter heißen:
links – Großmutter, rechts – Erklärung

9 Word search: parts of the body

P	C	A	P	F	U	B	T	O	E	S
A	A	R	E	O	H	F	K	K	A	T
W	T	M	J	O	Y	I	N	J	R	O
S	O	T	I	T	V	N	E	H	X	M
H	O	F	A	C	E	G	E	H	Y	A
O	T	N	T	I	C	E	E	Y	E	C
U	H	O	H	A	M	R	Y	X	R	H
L	E	G	R	N	O	S	E	R	G	D
D	A	H	O	F	U	S	H	A	N	D
E	R	E	A	S	T	M	H	A	I	R
R	T	O	T	Q	H	E	A	D	O	Q

arm, ear, eyes, face, fingers, foot, hair, hand, head, knee, leg, mouth, nose, shoulder, stomach, throat, toes, tooth
The secret word: *thermometer*

10 Lost words

1 never, *2* yet, *3* never, *4* just,
5 yet, *6* already, *7* ever

11 Word pairs

nod: head, **install**: software
cook: dinner, **pack**: suitcase
feed: animals, **wear**: pyjamas
ride: bike, **write**: report

12 Pronunciation

1 could, good, stood, would (ʊ)
2 art, heart, part, start (ɑː)
3 afraid, made, played, stayed (eɪ)
4 boat, note, throat, wrote (əʊ)

1 cook, *2* foot, *3* woman, *4* are,
5 chance, *6* laugh, *7* grey, *8* explain,
9 wave, *10* shoulder, *11* cold, *12* alone

The secret sentence: *Can you explain why the woman's shoulder hurts?*

13 Word ladder

sure, sore, more, move, love, live, life, wife

Unit 5

1 A German-English crossword

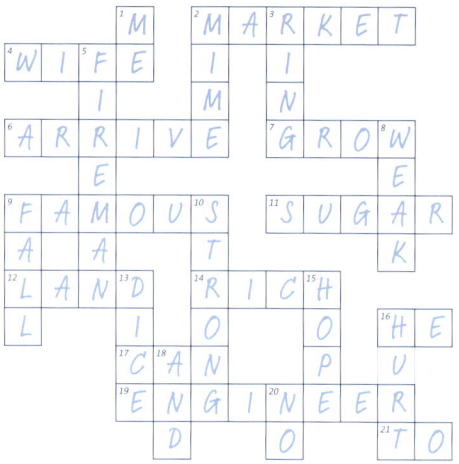

2 Spot the mistakes

1 idees: ideas, turist: tourist
2 no: know, hear: here
3 sience: science, exiting: exciting
4 slavs: slaves, tobbaco: tobacco
5 our: hour, enaugh: enough

3 Word snail

bought, rung, given, said, written, known, built, thought, gone, found, grown
The secret words: *Bristol tour*

4 Definitions

1 drink, friends – **pub**
2 help, doctors – **paramedics**
3 big, stay – **hospital**
4 small, pictures – **brochure**
5 sell, place – **market**
6 design, bridges – **engineers**

5 Word search

1 forest, *2* mountains, *3* tunnel, *4* statue,
5 heart, *6* dice, *7* thermometer, *8*, factory,
9 angel, *10* castle, *11* railway, *12* suitcase,
13 cow, *14* pyjamas, *15* sheep, *16* river

T	H	E	R	M	O	M	E	T	E	R	M
S	U	I	T	C	A	S	E	M	F	H	O
T	U	R	A	I	L	W	A	Y	A	Y	U
U	S	T	A	T	U	E	J	E	C	R	N
N	Y	Q	N	X	K	I	Z	L	T	C	T
N	N	U	G	E	T	I	C	E	O	C	A
E	O	F	E	A	N	F	Q	F	R	S	I
L	O	O	L	T	D	O	R	B	Y	H	N
H	E	A	R	T	M	R	I	C	B	E	S
P	C	A	S	T	L	E	V	Z	C	E	Y
P	Y	J	A	M	A	S	E	I	O	P	O
V	I	D	I	C	E	T	R	J	W	K	R

6 Odd word out
1 Bristol, 2 build , 3 family, 4 dice,
5 statue, 6 famous, 7 forest, 8 proud,
9 weather, 10 ill

7 Word families

Verb	Noun
build	building
listen	**listening**
drink	drink
describe	**description**
collect	collector
invite	invitation
copy	**copy**

8 Opposites
1 weak, 2 closed, 3 rich, 4 arrive,
5 beginning, 6 husband, 7 ill,
8 impossible

9 Numbers and letters
1 firemen, 2 teacher, 3 waiter,
4 engineer, 5 doctors, 6 singer,
7 policewoman, 8 shop assistant
The secret sentence: *When I'm older,
I want to be a star.*

10 Word friends
arrive: in Bristol, late
become: a singer, tired
grow: potatoes, fruit,
look: at me, sad
speak: to the teacher, too fast

11 What are the words?
1 something, 2 anywhere, 3 Somebody,
4 anybody, 5 anything, 6 somewhere

12 Word groups
places in a town: bar, café, cinema, department
store, pub, shop
food: hamburger, meat, orange, pizza,
popcorn, salad, strawberry
family: aunt, cousin, daughter, grandson,
husband, wife
rooms: bathroom, bedroom, dining room,
hall, kitchen, living room, toilet

Unit 6

1 Lost words
1 of, 2 for, 3 to, 4 till, 5 Between,
6 from, 7 in, 8 for

2 Odd word out
1 park, 2 round, 3 famous, 4 building,
5 London, 6 stone, 7 relax, 8 write

3 The fourth word
1 wear, 2 feet, 3 legs, 4 toes,
5 smell, 6 earache, 7 fog, 8 cool,
9 moon, 10 waitress, 11 driver,
12 harbour, 13 sad, 14 weak

4 Word web
1 every, 2 foggy, 3 dirty, 4 empty,
5 funny, 6 angry, 7 early, 8 happy,
9 today, 10 diary, 11 enemy, 12 ready

5 Words with different meanings
1 star: Stern, Star
2 before: bevor, schon mal
3 point: Punkt, zeigen
4 clean: putzen, saubere
5 walk: zu Fuß gehen, Spaziergang
6 open: Öffne, geöffnet
7 over: vorbei, über
8 move: Beweg, umziehen
9 round: rund, um ... herum
10 past: vorbei (am), Vergangenheit

6 Hour glasses
Die senkrechten Wörter in den Sanduhren
heißen: links – Termin, rechts – Großvater

1 B A D / 1 E G G
2 E M P T Y / 2 L A R G E
3 P A P E R / 3 H E A R T
4 C R O S S / 4 S U N N Y
5 B I G / 5 A D D
N / F
6 I T S / 6 M A P
7 R O M A N / 7 B A T H S
8 D R E A M / 8 O T H E R
9 M O N T H / 9 B L E E P
10 A T E / 10 A R T

7 Word search
1 drink, 2 catch, 3 scan, 4 build,
5 cross, 6 turn, 7 cycle, 8 sing,
9 have, 10 wear

C	Y	C	L	E	X	A	N	S	P
N	T	T	U	R	N	W	E	A	R
B	C	S	S	X	U	F	H	C	R
Q	R	F	W	B	U	I	L	D	A
S	O	Z	D	R	I	N	K	X	Y
Y	S	G	S	N	W	O	H	U	A
N	S	C	A	N	X	C	A	E	G
P	K	O	T	G	E	Q	V	F	H
W	G	W	K	Z	I	K	E	P	Q
T	S	I	N	G	C	A	T	C	H

8 What are the words?
1 must, *2* mustn't, *3* mustn't,
4 must, *5* needn't

9 Definitions
1 see, sky – **stars**
2 way, city – **map**
3 shop, buy – **department store**
4 stamps, send – **post office**
5 young, between – **teenager**
6 mistakes, change – **correct**

10 Word snake
1 **fly**: flew, flown
2 **feel**: felt, felt
3 **bring**: brought, brought
4 **choose**: chose, chosen
5 **teach**: taught, taught
6 **throw**: threw, thrown
7 **sing**: sang, sung
8 **speak**: spoke, spoken
9 **hide**: hid, hidden
10 **ride**: rode, ridden
11 **swim**: swam, swum
12 **read**: read, read
13 **put**: put, put
14 **sit**: sat, sat

11 Word ladder
need, feed, feet, felt, fell, fall,
ball, hall, hill, will, will, well

12 Word pairs
catch – ball
catch – thief
eat – lettuce
install – software
put on – clothes
read – brochure
scan – text
throw – ball

13 Pronunciation
1 cheer, dear, deer, here (ɪə)
2 bright, flight, quite, white (aɪ)
3 grew, threw, through, true (uː)
4 bought, brought, caught, sport (ɔː)

1 really, *2* beard, *3* disappear,
4 cycle, *5* behind, *6* IT, *7* move,
8 few, *9* proof, *10* install, *11* thought,
12 important

The secret sentence: *The man with
the beard disappeared behind the rhino.*

14 Picture puzzle
bath, lettuce, map, planet, star, stone,
tomato, wall

15 Crossword